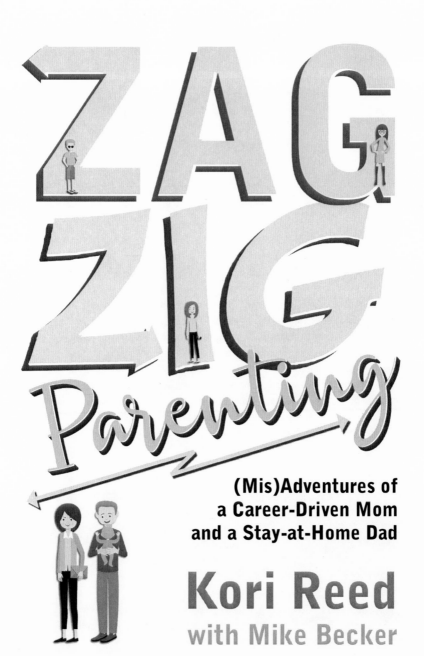

ZAG ZIG Parenting

(Mis)Adventures of a Career-Driven Mom and a Stay-at-Home Dad

Kori Reed
with Mike Becker

OMAHA, NEBRASKA

ZAGZIG PARENTING

Inquiries: www.ReedImagine.com

Library of Congress Control Number: 2017900515
Cataloging in Publication Data on file with Publisher

Paperback ISBN: 978-0-9725025-3-5
Kindle ISBN: 978-0-9725025-4-2
EPUB ISBN: 978-0-9725025-5-9

Publishing and Production: Concierge Marketing Inc., Omaha, Nebraska

Printed in the United States of America

10 9 8 7 6 5 4 3 2 1

To our children, Numbers 1, 2, 3, and 4,

You have taught us to be better parents, and so much more.

You gobbled up dad's infamous hot dog casserole and embraced mom's crazy picture poses with heart and soul.

We respect, appreciate, and love you to the core!

To our beloved Mimi,

who said it was okay to color outside the lines,
that the sky could be green,
and to always look on the bright side of life.

Contents

I'm a flipbook!

Flip my pages quickly to see these four in action!

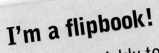

This is how we **F.A.M.I.L.Y.** Feel free to laugh, cry, and learn from our chaos.

Family, 2004

Family, 2016

Setting the Stage

When my sister took our then four-year-old, now twenty-something daughter to the zoo one day, they came across an exhibit where two giraffes walked side-by-side, one smaller than the other. My sister said, "Look at the mom and the baby hanging out together."

Our daughter looked at my sister with a confused expression and responded, "That's not the mom. It's the dad and the baby girl giraffe eating lunch together while the mom is away at work." Because, of course, that was her everyday worldview.

My sister laughed, and not knowing the anatomy of a giraffe to tell the difference anyway, agreed with her, and they enjoyed peacefully watching the "dad" and baby giraffe spend quality time together.

Of all the people in the world, we—my husband, Mike, and I—should have been the last ones to be perplexed by the observation of our preschool daughter. We should have celebrated the ease of her acceptance, but instead we paused, not sure if we should explain that not all would see it her way. We also weren't sure if opening her eyes to her unique view of our family would actually better prepare her for the world or protect her from someone who later may say she is silly to see it that way—even if they were not right to say that.

Since our first daughter was fourteen months old, and her sister was still an infant, Mike has been a full-time stay-at-home dad. We chose this situation for our family because we wanted to raise our kids this way, not due to a job layoff—we will get to more of that later.

Over the years, we've added two more kids—boys—and moved four times for my career opportunities; as it turns out, with each move and temporary time apart, we added a new child to the family. For the past two decades, Mike has been the primary stay-at-home parent to our now four adolescent and young adult children, two girls and two boys, each with their own personalities but all growing up in this nontraditional gender-role home.

For the past twenty-five years, I have been that career-driven professional, long before Facebook chief operating officer and author Sheryl Sandberg wrote her book encouraging women to "lean in" and stay fully engaged in the career track—regardless of future child-rearing decisions.

Mike and I have different views on life, and we are an example of opposites attracting; however, we are united by a trust in each other as well as the common goal and awesome opportunity to raise four kids to be the best people they can be. Mike will interject his viewpoint—along with comments from the peanut gallery—both in order to keep me honest and share a perspective of what it looks like to zag and then zig, when the majority of the population does the zigzag. Our intent is not to promote at-home parenting over all other parenting scenes, as we know many great working and at-home parents, but to praise all ways that families strive for work-life balance or, rather, integration—or, as we would say, finding joy in the chaos. As a working professional and mom I have experienced the heights of parenting joy as well as the depths of parenting perils, and share these vulnerable stories to connect and invite others to smile, laugh, and feel part of a parenting support club.

A passion for the zoo is part of our joy and has continued to be a favorite family activity from toddler years to teens and temperamental adults, and not just due to the unpredictable encounters with things from the wild, but in the broader animal kingdom, there are some standout examples of devoted dads and manager moms.

The lioness is the one who hunts and brings home the bacon while the king of the jungle sleeps during the day and fiercely protects his territory.

The male emperor penguin takes on the role of at-home dad and chief egg-warmer, after the female goes out to seek to restore nutritional reserves expended during the egg-laying process; he does not eat or move during the two months she is gone. If the chick hatches before Mom is back, he even feeds the chick with a curd-like substance from his esophagus.

Male flamingos are not only monogamous mates, they also help the mom select and build a nesting site *and* take turns incubating the eggs.

My ultimate favorite, though, and one that Mike likes to stay clear of, is the seahorse. Male seahorses are one of the only species known for male pregnancy; the mom deposits the eggs into the dad's pouch, and he fertilizes and incubates them for forty-five days until they are born as full, tiny seahorses.

MIKE: This is Mike, Kori's husband, friend, and dad to our four kids. I will interject my view throughout this book. Now, let's be clear about something here. I draw the line at the seahorse exhibit and won't even go see it with my wife. As much as she would have liked me to and I bet still wishes I could have carried one or more of our kids, it is not medically possible; and I am not convinced she fully comprehends that she can't will it to happen. She can get a lot done with her determination, but not this. I do love being a dad to our kids. I can't imagine raising them any other way, with me as the primary at-home parent, but I have no desire to carry them "in my pouch" or birth any babies. That is just too far.

These paternal instincts—in this case where the dad plays an integral role in raising the young—led to some interesting moments for us as professionals, parents, a couple, and a family; and we have lived this way the majority of our married life, well over twenty years.

Medically speaking, there are debates whether paternal instinct is a real thing, since, after all, Mom nurtures a baby for nine-plus months and releases the hormone oxytocin that increases kind, compassionate, and loving behaviors toward the life growing inside; while Dad's instincts are learned. On top of this, there are societal expectations, role models, and stereotypes that add a bit of pressure to the mix. In some cases, a full-time stay-at-home dad can be ostracized from working peers or praised for being a paternal anomaly, while the working mom can be ostracized for "prioritizing a career" over raising children and ridden with guilt about trying to succeed at both.

This is the paradox. We don't see articles in *Time* magazine asking, "Can men have it all?" or titles in *Newsweek* like "The Myth of the Perfect Dad." I don't often hear terms like the *daddy-track*, referring to men who choose to leave careers to raise families. Let me be clear here, I have no intent to disparage any dads out there who are fully engaged with their families—working outside of the home or in the home.

In 2015, *Time* did a piece about dad guilt, reporting on a Pew Research study which showed that almost half of working dads have guilt about whether they are doing enough, even though they report they spend more time with their kids than their own parents did. The female work population is growing. The same *Time* article reports about a third of pregnant women continued working throughout pregnancy in 1960, compared to more than 80 percent in the late 2000s; and in the same time period, women returning to work after pregnancy jumped by nearly 400 percent.

This is why we have seen such a surge over time in pop culture about working moms, the challenges of balance, being all to everyone, bringing home the bacon. Women have been managing work-life balance for years, and the trend is growing.

MIKE: While Kori and I chose this life, I can't say I went in willingly at first. I can validate that there are some differences as the at-home dad versus my female counterparts. While I have been excluded from some working-dad gatherings, I also have had the benefit of being the one that is different. As a room parent for the youngest child's elementary Valentine's Day party, I had divided the duties and I had a list of my own. My fellow room parents—who happened to be moms—called to check on me and make sure I had my list done, and when I told them what I had to do, they said they would take care of it for me. I was perfectly capable and had built time in my day to do these things: picking up cups, napkins, and beverages, but also did not object when they offered and did not feel too guilty about it. They offered. My wife, on the other hand, got frustrated at me, saying that would never have happened in the reverse.

At times, the guilt is what makes a mom go crazy on a quest for contentment, especially on the days when you feel you are not the mom, the employee, or the person you want to be. With child number two, I had taken a four-week leave, well before Yahoo CEO Marissa Mayer faced controversy over her short maternity leave. And, yes, at three weeks old my baby was in my office on Saturday, "playing" with her black and white toys while I typed away to catch up on email. (That was before working at home was all the rage.) You will read more stories about that situation and its impact.

Also, as my fellow working moms planned for at least three months of leave, if not longer, we could only afford the standard six-week disability leave for all four kids; with one spouse at home, we could not manage on the partial pay that kicked in after that time. With our decision as a couple to have my career be the primary family support, I had to, wanted to, and liked to succeed in the workplace. At the same time, I love my family and strive to be the best mom to my four kids, and spouse to my husband who was making trade-offs of his own. For me, just being there was not enough; I had to do more.

It is that guilt that drove me in the early 2000s to work with my sister to self-publish children's books about great dads and stay-at-home dads. During the morning and night train commute to and from Chicago for my job as a senior manager of communication at a Fortune 500 company, I wrote rhyming stories like *Daddy Does the Dishes: and Other Daddy Deeds*, a tale from an early-elementary child's perspective about Mom getting on the work train as Dad got her and her siblings ready for school; and *My Daddy Can Touch the Moon*, a story about the phase in life when kids think dads are the "bomb.com," inspired by the time our foursome, ages six to one, watched the Olympics and said, "Dad could do the men's gymnastics rings, no problem," as I smiled at their sweet, admiring innocence and silently laughed in the kitchen.

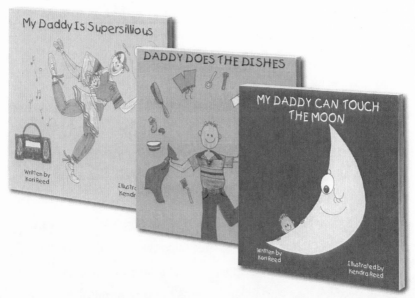

A passion for at-home dads inspires several stories.

MIKE: I am very fortunate that Kori wrote books about dads to give our kids a reassuring voice about their situation and as a compliment to me. She has always been supportive of a dad's role. I have to say that she and my sister-in-law put their own humor in the illustrations when our kids said, "My daddy can do that," in reference to the rings. My sister-in-law actually drew in the background my wife laughing. I am no wimp or a wallflower—maybe I can't hold the rings for as long as a professional athlete, but let's just say I don't get praised every day, and you will see that as the kids get older.

I wrote the stories so that our children would not think they were anomalies when the majority of their friends and characters in books and on television shows spent most of their days with Mom. I always have found books, songs, and poems to be cathartic at those times when you feel as if you are the only one in the world who feels a certain way.

When a song comes on the radio and articulates just the way you feel, you not only say, "Yes, that's it," but you also realize someone else might have felt that way if he or she wrote about it. For me, it was in reading the book *Dandelion Wine* by Ray Bradbury that I first realized I was not the only twelve-year-old to wake up to the world that day. The main character of the book is Douglas Spaulding, a twelve-year-old boy who starts the summer running through a field when he realizes he is alive, and he takes great joy in truly seeing—for the first time—all that is around him. It is a story about people's lives and what it means to live. I remember reading it and declaring to my mom that I was alive. While it became a family joke that lives to this day, reading about Doug at the time gave me a way to articulate my emotions, and I felt connected and less isolated. I wanted that same feeling for the family.

I had to make sure that my husband—a man among moms— felt no less important as a stay-at-home dad. I also wanted our kids, and their friends who read the children's books, to see that they might live in a house that is different from their friends, but feel no less loved. While I had and have utmost confidence in Mike as a dad, and had read studies on the positive influence of active dads in kids' lives, there were few longitudinal studies about the impact of a dad as primary caregiver while the mom worked in a progressively intense career, which meant travel, late-night deadlines, limited availability on weekends, and more.

I aspired for our children to feel a connection with others; to know they were not alone; they were part of a community, even if that community was pretty small at the time. Living the reverse from the norm can sometimes feel like a fish swimming upstream, kind of like that song from Sesame Street, "One of These Things Is Not Like the Others."

MIKE: When I first started staying home, I signed up for Mommy and Me classes, where the majority of attendees were moms and kids. As the only dad at daytime Kindermusik, I went right along when the instructors said, "Okay, moms, let's walk in a circle." Once I got over the fact that it was about the kids and not my ego, I rather enjoyed it and got a chuckle when some would correct themselves and say "moms and dad."

While we had some success with the business side of the self-published children's books, the kids got excited at seeing themselves in a real book. The local newspaper wrote an article about the books and featured my husband, which led to a photojournalist following him around for the day. That photographer was invited to have his pictures included in the photo book called *America 24/7*, a coffee-table-type publication from the creators of the *Day in the Life* series. It featured pictures from more than 25,000 photographers designed to create a vivid look into modern American life of experiences across the nation that happen within a week. On page 44 is a picture titled Mr. Mom; and in the state-specific version of the same style book, there are more pictures of the family. It was not about the short-lived fame, but more about the recognition for the family self-esteem that I valued.

Project "Book for Self-Esteem" was my night job, post-midnight, after the kids were in bed; work emails were done; we spent a little couples time during and after the news; and the house got quiet again.

During the day as a director of communication at a Fortune 500 company, I managed merger and acquisition communication, change initiatives including plant closings and division mergers, crisis situations including a plant shooting, and product recalls.

By day, I had become an ace at strategy, processing, and planning for large-scale change, union-labor negotiations, getting teams to align to a new direction, creating a business case to convince leadership to fund a new program, and vying with various departments for key resources. I liked it and was good at it. My bosses deemed me a high performer, and while I had some areas for improvement, my strengths as an achiever, communicator, and someone who took great responsibility led me to take on some challenging assignments.

Eventually, leadership asked me to direct all aspects of the company's citizenship, from running the company's foundation and multi-million-dollar, national charitable giving budget to developing the company's signature cause and acting as lead spokesperson. I traveled a lot, met and worked with some passionate advocates, and became an expert on the cause and corporate giving.

You guessed it. I had the proverbial candle burning at both ends—trying to be my best at everything I did and rarely feeling fully gratified at all aspects at the same time. As my career progressed, growing from manager, to senior manager, director, senior director and vice president, I also had become a master at disconnecting the pieces of my life. Each segment— work, kids, marriage, friends, and more—had its own neat little project plan.

Accordingly, some people at work did not know I had *any* kids let alone *four* of them, and some of my neighbors and friends knew I worked, but did not know what I did or that I was an executive. Some of my colleagues did not know I made sacrifices like they did and moved my family a few times, and some of my family did not know highlights from work—good or bad—whether I won an award or got chewed out by an exec for something that was not mine to manage.

MIKE: This was a challenge. When she came home, she did not want to talk about work at all. She drilled the kids and me about our day, every detail of it, and she might share a few nuggets of her day with us. After the kids went to bed, she was either back on email or too tired to talk about any adult stuff. I wanted to know more. I often spent the day discussing art projects, wiping noses, and grocery shopping. I wanted to hear how adults acted in the workplace. I wanted to celebrate the successes with her. When this didn't happen and she would fall asleep on the couch snoring, I was more than happy to change the channel to SportsCenter.

I even kept my name separate to protect the family in case there was any blowback—from the job or the books—on Kori Reed, so it would not affect the Mike Becker family. (It is the same reason why I refer to our kids in this book as Number 1, Number 2, Number 3, and Number 4. People can find out their names, but our kids have their own stories to live and tell.)

Okay, that did help me justify the reasons to Mike that I did not change my name, but the reality is that I never wanted to change my name. On top of that, my male boss at the time we got married had the name Becker, and I wanted no false pretense that this was a case of nepotism. As a female in a heavily male-dominated manufacturing work environment, I did not want to risk the potential doubt the same name may cause. I held my ground and stayed Reed, legally.

MIKE: When that boss moved on, and we even changed companies, I asked her to change her name to Becker, but she said the IRS already knew her as Reed, and it would be too challenging to go through all the paperwork. Note to my younger self: you may like the name of Kori Becker, but when she never wrote Kori Becker, even on the marriage class sign-in sheet, she was never going to change her name. It will be okay, but it is not going to happen as you thought.

The irony is that in my last five years as vice president, my job focused on integrating projects across the corporate matrix—something I did well. But I very much struggled to blend or harmonize any parts of my own life—even though the facts supported the benefits of integration. According to a recent article in the *International Journal of Psychological Studies* on work-life balance, one of many out there, separating work from personal life does prevent positive spillover for both.

I am not now boasting or proud of any of these behaviors, nor shameful. At the time, however, I have to admit that my picture of motherhood and my actions while away from work did not align. I was stressed, and as my career continued to bloom, I kept feeling under-successful in every segment, which is never a healthy state for a type-A person who is excessively ambitious with a sense of urgency.

When I did not live up to my ideal picture of being a mom, I overcompensated when I was in full-time mom mode. Our oldest child's third birthday included Mother Goose, Elmo, Barney (of course all look-alikes due to costume licenses), crafts, homemade cake, a piñata, and more. That was way overboard for the child who just wanted to go to bed when Elmo's look-alike showed up. Of course, I did not let her take her nap—as if I did not know the consequences of excessive overscheduling for a toddler.

Go ahead and laugh, as I now can at myself. Needless to say, what was intended to bring her great joy, ended in tears and tantrums for me while my daughter settled for a long night's sleep.

Now it is my time to write some stories and reconnect with fellow working parents. Many women have blazed trails before me, and in appreciation for that, it is my turn to "pay it forward"—to create a safe space for other parents who are either contemplating how to manage work and family, considering a working mom/at-home dad scenario, or who are currently experiencing high levels of stress or guilt living in the midst of day-to-day work-life integration and find themselves falling short of perfection, seeking wisdom in the chaos, and looking for contentment in the present.

This is exactly why I am writing this collection of authentic, vulnerable stories and inviting my husband to share his "outside" view—even though I am at high risk of seeming ridiculous at some moments in time. There are plenty more Elmo stories in my life. I hope these stories make you smile, feel relieved, and cry (with me), and that this is generally cathartic for you as busy people and parents who just want to do right—but who are sometimes not sure you are sane in the process. You are not alone.

The following stories capture the events I have encountered as a working professional and a mom, with an authentic viewpoint from a twenty-year at-home dad veteran. This is your invitation to be present, to learn to laugh at the moments in life that are surreal in nature—or just plain weird, to find a common ground to connect with others, to love yourself, and to just be. After all, that is what I am trying to do, at the risk of being extremely vulnerable with you, and this collection is part of my journey.

Mike and the four-pack on a
Sunday afternoon in the park.

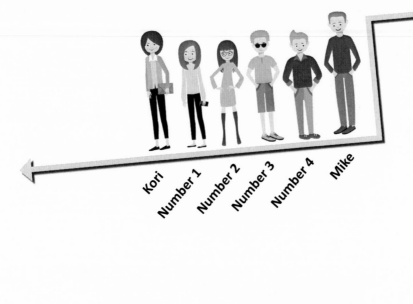

Kori Number 1 Number 2 Number 3 Number 4 Mike

Introduction: Our Story

It had always been my dream, my vision map since I was sixteen years old, to be a working mom with a stay-at-home husband and nearly a handful of kids. That was in the eighties when the phenomenon of working mom and full-time dad was just an anomaly, and the idea was popularized with actor Michael Keaton's performance as *Mr. Mom*.

Today, the trend is growing, but is still not the norm. Mike and I met in high school, late in our sophomore year, and he knew that about me.

MIKE: I told her, sure I would do it! Back then I would have said just about anything to make her happy. I was a sixteen-year-old boy with a crush, attracted to her for her drive, and loved the idea that I could golf during my days and not be constrained by a nine-to-five job. Also, I was a teenage boy who knew making my girlfriend happy led to some good makeout sessions for me. Little did either of us know then, well maybe she did, that her dream would become a reality—but not my daytime golf vision because raising kids is a full-time job and then some. As I look back now, I would have taken even once a week for golf, or even once a month!

Let me walk you through the speedy version of the long-term relationship that got us to where we are today. To say we were high school sweethearts used to make me gag, only because it wasn't as mushy as it sounds. At the time, I was editor of the high school newspaper, head of the pep club, captain of the softball team, and the high school mascot. In other words, I was considered your classic overachiever.

I wrote an editorial against P.D.A.—Public Displays of Affection—on school grounds. I confided in my husband—then boyfriend, who regretfully agreed to a morning handshake while on school grounds—that when I got married—and stressed, a long time from then—I wanted to work and have my husband stay at home and raise the kids. (My aunt didn't burn bras in the sixties for nothing.)

We wound up attending different colleges. Determined to be the next Katie Couric—then *Today Show* anchor—I went to the University of Missouri, the number-one journalism school in the nation. Mike went to Michigan State, pursuing a business degree in marketing. Yes, we were dating, but I was going to Missouri, and if he didn't want to go there, well bye-bye. We survived the long-distance relationship.

MIKE: She said I just kept hanging around long enough that she finally gave in.

I finished college a semester before him. He wasn't ready to get married; journalism jobs were few and far between at the time, and I had the opportunity to go to graduate school in Nebraska; again, I said bye-bye. Fast-forward, a year into grad school, we got engaged, and he moved to Nebraska. We married after grad school, got jobs, and three years later, we were expecting our first child.

Little did we know what was ahead....Chicago, 1993

MIKE: Wow, that really is a fast-forward! That is my wife, be direct and get to all the points fast; however, she is a romantic, but does not want to be seen as mushy, which means there is a lot to read between the lines, which at times makes marriage a very interesting, challenging journey. But I am in it for the long haul!

Phew, I summed up what seemed like a lifetime ago in two paragraphs. Life continued. Two months before our due date for baby number one, he told me that he didn't think he could give up his job to stay home. Now, hearing the way I approached life at the time—precisely determining my steps—I handled this decision with a calm, cool demeanor.

Oh, wait, wrong person. Now I remember. I freaked! Let me give a word of advice to any man or life partner out there; it is not wise to tell your type-A, seven-month-pregnant wife that her lifelong dream since she was sixteen years old has now changed and she would need to figure out a new plan B, and fast. There is no reason to rehash the past with details of that "lively discussion," charged by emotions and multiplied by pregnancy hormones. Suffice it to say, I have grown a lot in my ability to accept plan B, and with more grace. I didn't say total grace, but more grace than I did at that time. Experience brings wisdom; learning is another strength of mine, and I am still learning to this day.

MIKE: I can say this now: it was all about my ego. Sure, when we were sixteen I said I would stay home and a few times after that; however, when the time really came, when it was really about quitting my job, I could not do it. What would my dad think? What would I say to the guys? Would I be like Michael Keaton's *Mr. Mom* character and make a grilled cheese sandwich with an iron? I was raised an only child and, now, how would I be a full-time dad for a girl? When push came to shove, I did not go in willingly, but now, I am glad and would not change a thing. I got to be there for some of the biggest, most impactful milestone moments in life, from first steps to morning snuggles to hearing "Dada" for the first time!

Looking back, it was the best thing that happened to us and our daughter. We did not live near family; they were all states away from us. We had a wonderful day care lady, Miss Tammy, who helped us become better parents in the long run. As first-time parents, choking hazards like grapes were not even in our house, but the experienced Miss Tammy showed us how to expose our child to new things in a safe way. Tammy helped us get through the first time our daughter got bit by another child and, to my horror, the first and only time she bit another child. (By the time we had child number four, we knew biting could be a normal part of the toddler days).

Maybe, just maybe, I was a bit uptight with my first child, but Tammy was so successful in raising kids that I watched, learned, and listened; she was like a child whisperer. I look back on our day care time and not only appreciate it, but also better relate and respect working parents who chose childcare as an option and single parents who really have even fewer choices.

MIKE: She did eventually thank me for my decision to change her plans. Okay, that's a lie, but a man can dream.

I remember playing rock-paper-scissors with my husband when our daughter was too sick to go to daycare; we considered whose business meeting was more important or whose boss would be more understanding. Who could better bribe the other one? I highly respect dual-working and single-parent households that face these choices on a regular basis. I also respect many wonderful childcare providers and institutions that are part of family plans.

After about twelve months as dual-working parents, we had the opportunity to accept a transfer with my job, which required a move to the eastern part of the country. As a couple, we agreed it was the right move. We were expecting child number two at the time and—given our situation and a new location away from family—decided to try out Mike staying home with the kids and me going to work.

MIKE: Yes, I went kicking and screaming into this new role. I went on several job interviews and also tried to see if I could work remotely with my employer, but nothing was working out. Once I started interviewing day care providers, my choice was pretty clear, I was becoming a Mr. Mom, or the more politically correct term, a stay-at-home dad.

Another funny, notable thing happened on this journey—a blatant example of sexism. In the midst of the move, my wife had to work on the plant floor near our then current home because the union was on strike. Even though the company allotted three trips to find a house, the human resource leader would not approve the house-hunting trip for just me, saying he would never let a man buy a house without his wife seeing it. We had to because she could not leave. We fought it. I went and I did buy the house without her seeing it (she only saw Kodak pictures). At the time there were no virtual tours or high-quality-image smartphones either. Phew, she liked it.

The first year was rough in that Mike was the primary parent to the two kids, and I worked outside the home and did the other stuff, such as grocery shopping, making dinner, and cleaning the house. Every Saturday morning, I woke up early and nag-nudged him to work together to clean the house. Mike hated it. The stress highlighted the opposite traits in both of us. I like order, and he is okay with clutter. I like to plan ahead, and he likes to be in the moment. All in all, we were both stressed.

Between the lack of sleep from a new baby and new lifestyle, there was little time to be a couple. At that time in life, we could not afford a housecleaner that many couples turn to for sanity—later in life we did.

On a family vacation, I read a book called the *Family Manager* by Kathy Peel. After I finished reading it, I handed it to my beloved spouse and said, "You've been promoted! You are now the 'family manager,' and here are your duties." While it has worked out, I don't recommend treating your husband this way. Again, I have matured in the way I handle plan B. A few apologies and a few years of marital counseling later, we created a better sense of balance and role clarity to the point that he has been the primary family manager for nearly two decades.

Let me set the record straight. He is not a Mr. Mom or a House Dad. He is a dad, and he is very much a man who wears the pants, drinks a few beers on occasion, and watches ESPN way more than I want him to. He cooks and does a mean load of laundry, but he does not see dust or clutter the same way I do. While he can easily handle a roomful of moms at Kindermusik class, he is more comfortable hanging with the guys and talking about fantasy football and baseball. He juggles the kids' schedules, but doesn't always remember what I asked him to do yesterday.

MIKE: I also don't always get the schedule correct either. For all intents and purposes, we are a normal couple that has its own conflicts and challenges raising our family. The only difference is that when my neighbor talks about the boss who whines about deadlines, expects more from him every day, and leaves a mess for him to clean up, I can relate, but my bosses at some point were under four feet tall and referred to me as Dad. I wonder if my attention to some details will be discussed later. Who am I kidding? Of course they will be. Over the years, I have given Kori a lot of good material that she can respond to.

I am a woman who loves and respects my husband. I like pantsuits, especially when I can wear a killer pair of shoes, and I love to shop for shoes. I worked outside the home full-time, but also wielded my God-given mother's intuition on a number of occasions to save the day for family happenings. While I am no Betty Crocker, I can bake a mean batch of chocolate chip cookies. I love chick flicks, and I have checklists galore, from kids' after-school routines to family rules and more.

All in all, I am a woman, and he is a man. But for the majority of our kids' childhood, I was a woman working in a male-dominated work world, and he was a man thriving in a female-dominated at-home world. In general, we didn't think about our genders and just did what we needed to get done. Here is an example of how this plays out in our household:

Years ago, my husband and I were having a very lively discussion in the kitchen about roles and duties in the family.

In short, he was upset that I spent way too much time at work, and I was upset that he didn't understand or appreciate the pressure I was under as the breadwinner. He was quick to point out to me that he was much more of an active dad than our friend Rod. It was true.

When Rod went home after work, he sat on the couch and watched TV while his wife made dinner, watched the kids, and got backpacks ready for the next day. My husband was absolutely right. Mike was and is an extraordinary dad, managing the schedules of four children, making sure homework is done, dinner is on the table, and any TLC (tender love and care) is delivered at regular intervals throughout the day. A number of my girlfriends frequently tell me how lucky I am that he is so involved with the family, cleans the house, cooks, and does the laundry. I am very grateful.

Mike's smug grin, however, forced me to play the reverse card. I told him there was no denying that he was way more of an involved-dad role model than Rod, but in our family roles, I would be the one to compare to Rod and he would be the one to compare to Rod's wife, Sylvia. As you might imagine, Sylvia was a stay-at-home mom who tried to do it all. She vacuumed the house every day, made sure the kitchen counter space was always clean and available, her kids were always well-groomed, and she also had time to be the room mom and lead the Parent Teacher Association. My husband is awesome at a number of things. Keeping counter space clear or a sink empty of dirty dishes? Not so much.

MIKE: First, there is a spot for everything! Next, okay, I had to give in to her on the Rod comparison. I mean, I like Rod; he is a great friend. A lot of times, when the kids were younger, I envied his quiet time on the couch before dinner. This is often the witching hour for all families, you know, the time when the after-school snack has worn off and dinner is not ready yet. That is not my favorite time of day with the kids. I would love to be like Rod in this case and just catch up on the news or relax so that I can prepare to manage the rest of the night with homework and more. When I first started staying home with the kids, I remember getting excited when the garage door opened so that Kori could take over kid duty and I could have a minute to myself. I didn't care what was going on in her world at that moment, I just needed to escape mine for a few minutes.

As a side note, we have many friends who are dual-working couples, manage extremely well, and at the same time have their own struggles when it comes to business travel. We have male friends who work and are quite active in child-rearing, as well as friends who are female professionals who work full-time and act as the primary parent, arranging doctor visits, meal planning, and after-school care. We have friends who are single parents, who, Lord knows how they do it all.

I have admiration for all family styles. I have been the primary breadwinner, and my husband has been the primary stay-at-home parent, which means I can often relate to and empathize with a working spouse who misses a birthday party or other key events in a family due to work, and Mike can connect with a spouse/partner who has made a well-planned and executed dinner for the family, with one plate that sits in the microwave for hours, maybe even until the next day (until I get to it).

We have lived in these roles for so long, we, for the most part, no longer see it as different, until we talk about the Rods of the world or encounter moments in life that deviate too far from the norm, especially living in upper-middle-class areas where a number of families have at least one stay-at-home spouse, mostly moms. There are a number of moments we encounter along our journey, attempting to balance work and home, and these stories are authentic to the problems, the joys, the challenges, and the pathetic attempts at times to justify some action or inaction as parents in the process.

Regardless of your path to success—working parent, stay-at-home parent, single parent—enjoy the moments when your child can look beyond the stereotypes, the role expectations, and reverse-role expectations to see a dad giraffe—or aunt, uncle, nanny, or grandparent, for that matter—hanging out at the zoo with his kid.

From the greats who pass before us comes the wisdom of the ages, and this is one from my mom, who lived seven full decades but passed all too soon. When we colored outside the lines as kids, she would say, "Lines are just suggestions." May you find wisdom coloring your own picture book along the way and not be confined by the lines of life others have established.

Comments from the Peanut Gallery: Child Number 1 (the oldest)

Who knew the watermelon bowl made a good hat? July 4, 2005

Number 1 cleans up well for homecoming dance. 2012

It's good to finally be back in the spotlight after eighteen years of having to share all the love and attention with the other three. This is Number 1, the first and the finest of the Becker bunch. I always complained about how my parents felt the need to have more children after having me, but I have come to realize that I was so great they kept trying to make copies of me. Little did they know I am one of a kind.

All joking aside, on the list of things most important to me, family comes right after my connection with the Lord. I would rather stay home with family than do just about anything else; however, me being highly introverted with a tendency to be lazy accounts for a large part of my homebodiness. Seriously though, my family means the world to me. Typical gender roles and specific stereotypes do not apply to the Becker household;

we are simply too cool. Though my upbringing may have been nontraditional, I think my siblings and I have turned out okay.

None of us, so far, have ever had any trouble with the law (except Number 2 who had a car accident and has gotten a speeding ticket). I have remained on the dean's list throughout high school and now for several years in college and will publicly say, "I love you" to my parents, no matter who hears me. All these examples and more prove there is no one perfect way to parent. Don't get me wrong, none of us is perfect: my parents still fight; my dad will forget lots of my mom's priorities; my mom never remembers my friends' names; and I get *hangry*— the combination of hungry and angry, which often leads to fights with my parents over silly things because I need to eat. However, somehow we make it all work. It's all about making it work, isn't it?

At a young age, I always felt responsible for my siblings. With my mom gone a lot for business and my dad being a "guy," I felt responsible to "mommy" and protect them. I would and will do anything for Numbers 2, 3, and 4 and hope they never forget that. Our bonds have been made stronger through making fun of our dad's "creative" casserole combinations and complaining about mom's need for control of every situation including her desire for us to always be close and be there for one another. Though our personalities differ greatly, we all know how amazingly blessed we are.

At the center of this great family are Mom and Dad, Kori and Mike, madre y padre. They are the definition of opposites attract. I always knew they liked each other, but when they were arguing about who forgot Number 4's tap shoes or why

the time of Number 2's choir concert was scheduled at the wrong time, or why Mom couldn't get to Number 3's basketball game on time, I would question if they really loved each other, but as they would kiss in front of us kids, as they did quite often, it always put any question like that to rest.

They have been together since their sophomore year of high school and just can't seem to get enough of each other, good or bad. Somehow after all this time they are still the dynamic duo. Though I don't always agree with their parenting decisions and tend to make my opinion quite clear as my mother likes to point out, I still think they are the best ones out there.

My mom and dad have known each other for over half of their lives. They became happy parents of four wonderful kids. There have been so many memories over the years. There have been tears, disappointment, successes, and cheers. Through all the ups and downs and all the life lessons, they have been there for all of us. No matter what, we always know that both of them have our backs and will be there for us. I am so grateful for my parents and the amazing life they have created for my siblings and me.

1

The year I put our three-year-old on a work-related Performance Improvement Plan (PIP) and nearly lost my job as mom

As a working mom of four now adolescent and young adult children, I have been challenged in my ability to integrate work and home life, with the exception of one area, and that is the drive to continually improve performance of the team, which I often will interchange with "family" when I am home.

MIKE: Much to our joy—and yes I am being sarcastic. We will talk more about my feelings regarding her using her "work" tools on her personal relationships. It is a challenge for which she often needs intervention.

As a manager at an early age, I developed a high competence at setting a goal and working toward that goal, recognizing that a 10 percent improvement over last year would become next year's baseline.

When I was communication manager in a 2,000-employee, union-operated manufacturing plant, we had an annual audit that prescribed best practices, ranging from employee communication on all three shifts to working with the media and outside community to managing plant leadership communication and working closely with the union leaders on a regular basis. We were rated against those standards and then crafted an improvement plan for the next year. With one of my strengths identified from Gallup's Clifton StrengthsFinder® assessment as ACHIEVER, I am driven by the need to accomplish something every day in my work outside the home. The home team created a lot of scenarios for me to practice this skill with precision.

MIKE: Yeah, that is not me.

From the time we are born, we are rated on a performance scale, and it continues throughout life. The first is the Apgar score, a measure of the physical condition of a newborn infant, obtained by adding points for heart rate, respiratory effort, muscle tone, and so forth. A score of 10 is the best possible condition. Then, throughout childhood, there are the developmental wellness visits where a child's growth (height, weight, head circumference, for example) is measured according to the percentile within the population. Then there are third-grade reading levels, high school rankings—you get the point.

I am not critical of these frameworks, as they are designed to monitor health, growth, and progress as well as determine if interventions are needed. Throughout life, these measures become a norm by which we rank progress.

All good things, to an extreme, however, can become detrimental to the self-esteem for one and bragging rights for the other. Take my son, for example, who, when I told him he and his brother both had a head circumference in the 90th percentile, decided he and his brother were, of course, the smartest ones in the family; my oldest daughter, on the other hand, who was old enough to understand the birds and the bees and the birth canal said, "Ouch, mom!"

Performance and rating scales can be very effective for those who are type-A or extremely achievement-oriented or just want to do and be the best. For others, though, scales should come with warning signs like those medication commercials you hear on television: "X could cause nausea and excess loose stools in some patients; if you break out using X, stop using X as it could be a sign of a fatal reaction."

Here is the commercial I might write for performance scales: "For those who strive for near perfection or think good is just not enough, use rating scales at your own risk; if you get hives when you can't check every box off a list or if your child gets a 95 percent but you know she can get at least a 97 percent or if you continually push yourself to achieve more, look away from the scale; take an aspirin and a time-out to meditate."

MIKE: Please, yes, meditate more.

Here's what happens when high-achieving mom meets preschool performance scales. When our daughter was in preschool, about three years old, she brought a report home that said she was a little behind on scissor skills. Mike looked at the report and saw all of the other glowing reports on social skills and early math; he celebrated with a high-five and then a big hug with my daughter. I, too, gave the congratulatory hug, but then told her we would work on her scissor skills each night.

Now, let me preface that my day-to-day training was all about improvement. Anyone who has worked in a situation where performance ratings are the norm knows the system highlights improvement areas. In my experience in Fortune 500 companies, there is a list of priority behaviors, and a person is ranked on a five-point scale: (1) Exceeds, always going beyond; (2) Meets-plus, doing what is expected plus more; (3) Meets, you are doing what is asked; (4) Meets-minus, you are sometimes doing what is asked; and (5) Below, you are not meeting performance standards.

I have managed a few people who have been on the lower scale and had to implement a PIP, or Performance Improvement Plan, that lays out clear expectations and consequences if goals are not met.

It was only natural for me to assess a "team member's" performance and put a plan of action in place for our three-year-old after I saw her performance scores—I mean, preschool progress report. I drew five lines on each paper, and, at night for the next week or so, the idea was for Number 1 and me to cut together and talk about the day.

At first she was excited. After dinner we cleared the table, got the paper and scissors, and started cutting. The first few minutes it was going great, and then it happened. After cutting the third line, she set down her scissors and she was done. From my standpoint, there were still two more lines on the page that she needed to cut, so she needed to return to the table to finish her project.

Before I could interject, Mike decided that a three-year-old did not need to cut straight lines. He intervened, told her to go have fun playing, and took the scissors from me.

MIKE: I took the scissors because the look of bewilderment on her face in reaction to someone not finishing a clearly designed task—even a three-year-old—scared even me. I was not sure about her next move and decided to take the family's safety into my own hands. Number 1 is great with scissors now, by the way. Luckily I came out of this incident unscathed. Looking back on it now, I can't believe I survived or at least wasn't put on my own PIP.

I am sure my husband will say this, so I will beat him to the punch: I love scales and frameworks. I am competitive in that I like to do the best I can. I don't need to be king of the mountain, but I do strive for a personal best; and, like most type-A people, I occasionally have a hard time understanding why people settle for okay, when they really have the capacity to be more. In the case of the scissors, I will concede that our three-year-old did not need to practice daily.

MIKE: Well, as usual, she beat me to it! We are both competitive, but one of us might be considered an overachiever, extraordinarily motivated, responsible, and highly driven. My mother-in-law, a hard worker who loved to have fun, even told her daughter to loosen up. When my wife had a report card with all A's, her mom would say, "Great! Next time you can have a little more fun and get a B." I did well and was okay with a B.

I like the way writer and author Shawna Niequist, in her book *Present over Perfect*, describes present as fresh bread—lumpy and warm—and as a face bare of makeup; I would describe it as lines on a paper that are not perfectly cut by a toddler. I still push for improved performance among my "team," but I am opening my eyes more and more to the idea that being present in the struggle is a big step toward momentous improvement over time.

Number 1, all smiles and wrapped in a bow. Dec. 1999, Virginia

Work voodoo in the home: Binders, brazen influence, the bodacious X, and backing off

There are times in life when you are so caught up in the excitement of things that you are too close to read the danger signs that are flashing everywhere, especially in front of your face. I should have noticed those warnings a lot sooner, before I had thoughts of insubordination in reference to my family. After all, my actions had results in other settings (work), and clearly I thought the home team—my family—should follow my lead.

When our second child was born, I returned to work after four weeks to help manage and navigate one of the biggest problems the plant had faced in years—a potential work stoppage as the union opposed a change in work schedule that would make the company more efficient and change employees' schedules and ways of life, including working Sundays in the northern edge of the bible belt of the country.

It was an intense time, and one for which my training, experience, and relationship-building skills served as a valuable

asset. After the leadership team had reached an impasse with the union, they turned to me for ideas, and I created a strategy that allowed management to open volunteer lines of communication, while respecting union-management labor negotiation rules. The success of that strategy is one reason the vote passed, and, shortly thereafter, management asked me to move to headquarters and lead all plant communication.

Despite that win, I have to admit that my colleague, Tom, had a much better and consistent success rate at selling ideas to the plant manager. I highly respected Tom and his skills; I just did not know his secret—how he got his proposals through four times out of five, while I was batting around 0.300, above average in baseball, but not at an incredible rate.

One day I asked him, and he showed me his secret. He put our presentations side-by-side: mine, a stack of papers with data analysis and a business case; his, in a clean binder with page protectors, data presented in visual pie charts, and clear checklists for next steps. Don't get me wrong, there was substance behind his work, and I learned a valuable lesson about not only creating a solid, informed presentation, but also sharing it in a way that built confidence in the people I wanted to influence.

I honed my skills by attending more training throughout my career, including Sandy Linver's Speak and Get Results. The premise was that you start with your X statement, which is your destination—where you want your audience to be, or what you want them to say or do after you talk with them, and then build your talking points to get people there. It inspired me to practice more, and then I realized I had a ripe place to practice this behavior—at home with my husband. The training had a certain formula to it, and, at the time, we, as a couple, were dealing with some pretty big issues navigating marriage, kids, and a household. Of course, I wanted Mike to see it my way.

MIKE: Many years later this is still a sore topic for me, and I have coined the phrase, "Do not 'workize' me." I hate conflict with a passion; Kori thrives on it, and she is good at communicating her viewpoints. I am not a fan of calendars, charts, and organizational tools, yet each year she buys a new family planner to attempt to keep our lives informed and "neatly packaged." At home, she talks about project plans, "A" priorities, and goal-setting, like we are an organization to be managed. We are a family, and no binder or X statement can help us avoid a toddler crying and needing a long hug at 7:56 a.m. when she needs to be at day care by 8:00 a.m. or the importance of letting a preschooler tie his own shoes even if we are five minutes behind schedule that day.

I did extremely well in the class with business examples, but at home, Mike did not respond the same way my training role-play partners did. Maybe it worked a few times, but then he caught on quickly and said things like, "Save your manager tone for the office," or "The kids did not mean to spill on your neatly designed chore chart," (Although, I am not sure the kids at that young age had developed a taste for his favorite, Mountain Dew) or, best yet, "Oh, I thought you meant to recycle that to-do binder since it was sitting on the counter."

MIKE: I plead the fifth here—no comment for fear it may incriminate me or the kids.

I then created neatly color-coded to-do lists, similar to the ones I used in my office; although this time, I taped them to the cabinets at eye level—no spills and no recycling in that spot. To my dismay, when I returned home, none of the items were checked off the list. I created house project plans, not using the Gant charts we did at work, but lists for each room in the house, and, guess what, they were ignored too. Not ready to give up, I tried another leadership tactic, involving the family team in creating the plan and chore charts. There were some signs of improvement, but not near a "Meets" performance.

Then my face showed the expression of a perplexed, angry manager, who wondered, *Why didn't my team complete any assigned tasks?* My husband's face looked very similar, and he had a red glow on his cheeks with a slight irritation in the tone of his voice. "We are your family, not a project to be managed or staff you can boss around!" exclaimed the angry man with his little minis standing behind him.

That's the day I realized that work-life integration is not always beneficial for all, although I do still have an affinity for binders and a good paper checklist, even well after we all operate on virtual Google calendars.

Here is the dream—a Norman
Rockwell Family, 2003

Here is real life—chaos and shenanigans,
eyes closed and laughter. (Not pictured, mom
yelling pose commands) Omaha, 2010

Featured in this chapter:

Kori

Mike

Number 1

Number 2

The bathroom as a tranquil sanctuary and getaway place, despite the germs and flushing

3

One thing I bet a lot of moms can't say, that I can, is that our daughters have spent more time in men's bathrooms and locker rooms than most, starting at a very young age. I am not boasting at that one, I just think it is funny that Number 1 and Number 2 have vivid memories of following Dad around in the men's locker room at the local YMCA as young kids. It is just one of those gender issues we don't think twice about until someone tells the story, and then we say, "Oh, that's what happens when Dad is primary parent during the day."

MIKE: When the kids were all under six years old, I really did not have a choice. I did not feel like our kindergarten child was old enough to take care of herself and her preschool-age sister on her own. With a rambunctious two-year-old brother in the

mix and an infant boy to follow, I needed to monitor them all as we got ready for swimming lessons. I was always in a zone-defense mode, and, often, the only defender during the day when the kids were running the fast break. There were not a lot of kids in the men's locker room, let alone girls, and there was only one time a man politely suggested that the girls were old enough to use the women's locker room to which I said, "No, they aren't," so they followed me.

When Number 1 and Number 2, two years old and six months old, spent hours in the men's public bathroom at the grocery store, I have to say I initially questioned Mike's parenting qualifications. Mike reluctantly told me the story at dinner that night. He was at the grocery store with the girls, and, on this day, the six-month-old was really cranky. It had started that morning and continued.

While Number 1 was at school, the rest of the gang and Dad tackled the grocery store duties.

He took the girls to the bathroom to change the little one's diaper, thinking that was what she needed. Of course, back then, not a lot of men's bathrooms included changing tables. He laid the changing pad from the diaper bag down on the floor. (I still shiver when I think about it, but at least he put something down.) As soon as he laid her down, she stopped crying. He changed the diaper and picked her up to put her back in the front-facing baby carrier, and she started crying again. He laid her down again—on the changing pad, he stressed to me—and she stopped crying. At that point, she was happy.

I could tell he wanted to end the story there, but pressing through my fear that my two baby girls spent hours in the men's public bathroom, on the floor no less, I had to know more. After more probing, he said they spent an hour there. It was the first time all day that child Number 2 was happy, and he was enjoying the moment of peace. I dared to ask what our two-year-old was doing in the men's bathroom for the hour, and he said running around and playing. UGGHH!

MIKE: I really did not want to tell my wife about the bathroom day. She has a way of dragging stories out of me, and I wasn't fast enough to fake another story. She sniffed out the potential lie when I hesitated. I see it in our boys now, how she knows there is a story coming that is about half true. At that moment, I would have done anything to make my girls feel happy. Yes, I suppose, most moms would not have let their girls hang in the bathroom, and I did not make it a practice, but it was a peaceful moment for all of us. And when she said I let Number 1 run around and play, I meant that she and I played games that didn't involve touching anything to do with a toilet.

I can say that I have hidden out in a bathroom from time to time as a sanctuary from work, in the only place where a male boss could not follow me when I had had it and was on the verge of tears. While I am not a teary person, in general, there are fewer than a handful of times in my career that I have cried at the office. It is so frustrating for us females, and I am stereotyping, that extreme frustration or anger can start as tears. There are signs it is coming—the quiver in the voice, emotions welling inside that you want to push down in the moment, but they keep rising.

When I was a director of communication for a division of the business, I created and advised the president on town hall meeting content. He wanted a unique message concept, and I delivered a multimedia presentation that was both motivating and impactful. I could tell he was not totally comfortable, but he agreed to the format. The day of the meeting, he did not follow the script and went off on a tangent and publicly ridiculed me for the lack of content effectiveness. I was furious at the lack of respect; if he did not want to do it, I would have suggested a different path, but he had agreed and then hung me out to dry when he decided, in the midst of it, that he really did not like it.

Within an hour after the end of the meeting, I had to get on a company plane with him to the corporate office. I had to regain my composure before then. His ego was big enough that chastising him on the plane, in front of other colleagues, would have been political suicide, and if I let him know that this bothered me, he would have continued to pick at me like an itchy scab just waiting to come off a deep gash. I could not go back to my office cube, as talking to anyone at that point would have caused a relapse in the water works.

So there I sat, in the bathroom stall, for a long time. Of course, I put toilet paper on the seat and sat there. I made it through the rest of the day, and the next morning he and I had a productive follow-up conversation.

MIKE: Okay, now I don't miss those work moments, although I have challenging bosses, and I have been known to hide in the bathroom too. My bosses, however, don't have an appreciation for boundaries. If I don't lock the door, they walk right in, and if I do lock the door, they stand there and have a conversation through the door, whether it is resolving a sibling argument or asking what snack they can have. I finally had to teach them that a closed door means no business or Daddy will close down if he can't do his business.

Like my daughters in the men's locker room, I have been the lone female in a male-centric domain. Early in my career, I was often the only female in a leadership meeting and the only woman on a company plane, heading toward a manufacturing plant in a remote location. I have been the first female to explain to a boss I respected that he can't ask about a potential candidate's pregnancy status during an interview because it is considered a disability by most U.S.-based companies. I have been the only person to lean forward, in a room full of men that were senior to me, when the CEO asked, "Who wrote this?" even after all of the men approved it. I have been the only person in the room when a big, burly manufacturing plant manager broke down in tears when he had to tell the

employees whom he saw every day that the plant would close and they may lose their jobs.

There is an advantage to being the only female in those settings; you never have to wait in line for the women's restroom.

MIKE: And a shout out to all the men out there who have had to navigate the urinal with a child in a front baby carrier so that you can unzip and do your business without getting anything on your kid. It is a little surreal to look down into the eyes of your four-month-old daughter as you are peeing. We dads have our challenges too.

Sisters, 1998

Dad's girls, 2011

4

My hopes are dashed that my husband will change his ways: Rereading the "turn-of-the-century family journal" is proof that some things have stayed the same

With all fours kids coming to life around the turn of the century, Mike and I decided to keep a journal of our day-to-day activities in the year 2000—serving both as a once-in-a-lifetime-event memento as well as a family memoir. At the time the newly-computer-reliant nation worried about a phenomenon called Y2K and the looming computer crash that was predicted when the clocks changed and the dated-data switched from 12/31/1999 to 1/1/2000. With all of the media hype, we decided it was as good a time as any to document what we did in 2000 so that the kids had a record of their young lives, news, and fashions. This was pre-Number 4. Sorry kid.

MIKE: Again, love how my wife says "we." It was her idea, and I went along. I did the majority of the journal entries, as it happened also to be the year that my wife got a new job at a new company, and we moved, lived apart for a while, and she did some additional travel.

As I recently looked back on the journal entries, I smiled at some memories, laughed at others, and got a little teary at some of the items Mike wrote. He penned emotional entries about missing me while I was away on business trips—that year, work travel included quick trips to Argentina, Venezuela, and Brazil. We also lived apart when he wrapped up things in one state while I started a new job in another.

He wrote about his day-to-day travails of taking the girls to swimming or music class or Number 3 to the allergist. Then, after skimming nearly half the journal, I noticed another thing that was not so sweet, but also made me teary. I saw some traits in my spouse that perhaps annoy me today—and I have been trying to change for a while—but have been around since the turn of the century and before. Have I been arguing about these same things for this many years? Well, that is for another story.

MIKE: I keep telling her this is who I am, but she insists I can improve on these traits: forgetfulness, thinking my picture of a straightened house is good enough, or not worrying about what the kids wear as long as they are covered up on all the right places. She gets out her project plan template. I roll my eyes and say, "This is who you married, baby, and you love all of me, right?"

Here is a smattering of entries from Mike and me that may give you a peek at our lives with three kids, a move, lives apart, managing role reversal, and the turn of the century.

KORI, Jan. 14, 2000

Mike took the kids to the library, and the librarians helped him pick out a picture book called *The Father who had 10 Children*. It is a children's book by Bénédicte Guettier about a father who had ten children and every day made them breakfast, helped them get dressed, drove them to school, etc. One day he needed a rest and left the brood with grandma, but, after one peaceful day, he felt he was missing something ten times. Because it is so rare these days to have a stay-at-home dad, Mike can be kind of a stand out. It is nice to have a book to share with the kids that shows a dad as a caregiver.

MIKE, Feb. 7, 2000

Kori went to Canada today. She had to help out with the hiring of a new employee. That leaves me to care for the kids 24/7… alone. Always get a little nervous when I know I have to do it all. At the same time, I think I accomplish more because of it…

KORI, Feb. 21, 2000

Another funny story from today, [Number 2] likes to put a silk scarf on like Mommy does, closes the bedroom door and says, "Bye-bye, I am going to work!" She will come right back in the room and do it again. It is pretty cute and of course I feel guilty about leaving my kids to go to work, but I hope I am setting a good example.

[NUMBER 1], March 13, 2000
(written by Kori as she was too little at the time)

This is my first picture of my daddy—I don't know how to draw people without pigtails. Daddy would it be okay if I drew you with pigtails because I don't know how to draw your hair. (Fast forward to November 17 of that year, she draws Mike without pigtails).

Number 1 only knew how to draw pigtails for hair, even on Dad.

Dad loses pigtails! November 2000.

MIKE, March 16, 2000:

Today was just a normal activity day. [Number 1] had swimming and [Number 2] and I played with the basketballs in the gym until her Kindermusik class. After lunch, it was time to go to the doctor. Turns out [Number 3] needed one shot and [Number 1] needed three shots. [Number 3] cried for a minute and then took a bottle; while [Number 1] took two shots in one arm and then, when the nurse said it would sting, she cried and wanted me to hold her for a while…later that night Kori had a dinner meeting with a colleague.

MIKE, March 26, 2000

The next chapter in our lives happened today when Kori left on a plane to start training for her new job. She will fly home on Tuesday night. On Wednesday, we drive to the new city to house hunt, and on Friday I will go with my buddies to the annual "Boys Weekend."

MIKE, May 3, 2000

Today was relatively light in terms of activity. Took the girls to school in the morning and then came home for the "Big Garage Sale." I say that with a big laugh; our neighbor said it

was the best day for a sale, and, while I don't agree, she is a really nice older woman who runs the neighborhood. All the neighbor kids came by, and I ended up giving a lot of stuff away for free.

MIKE, May 4, 2000

Kori comes home this weekend (from commuting to new job in new state). I am very excited and I can't wait for her to get here…in the afternoon [Number 2] and [Number 3] took naps and I made [Number 1] rest too. While they rested, I worked to get this house in order. Don't get me wrong, I kept the house straightened, but my wife and I have a different standard of what clean is. With her here for only two days, I want her stay to be stress-free.

KORI, May 10, 2000

I am in town for Mother's Day weekend. Let me tell you that I miss the kids and Mike. When I am away from them, I block it from my mind so that I don't think about it, but when I see them, I know why people say home is where the heart is. There is something very right about being a family… how they change in a short time. I have been wondering lately if we are doing the right thing, making this move. This transition has been difficult—but we will be a family again, in the same spot, soon.

MIKE, June 8-10, 2000

Kori was not here for the days of dance dress rehearsal, and I wasn't going to try to put [Number 1]'s hair in a bun, so I took her to a hair salon to have it done. I can't believe how well they did…Kori and her sister were driving in for the show, but I needed help with hair and make up again, so back to the salon we went.

MIKE: As a side note, not in the journal, the movers packed Number 1's hairpiece that day, after dress rehearsal and before the actual recital. I could not tell Kori. I ran around all day trying to duplicate the exact hairpiece—phew, it worked. We found the actual, original hairpiece after we unpacked at the new house, in a new state, well after the dance recital.

MIKE, July 18, 2000

This morning was a busy one. Kori left for a business trip this morning. First, she went to work. Then took a taxi to the airport and flew to a plant operation in Iowa. She will be back tomorrow after work. When I woke up, [Number 2] had crawled next to me in bed and [Number 1], still preschool in age, was dressed and ready to go for an adventure with a

friend. [Number 2] and I got ready for her special week with Grandma. After the girls went on their separate adventures, [Number 3], my son (in his car seat) and I did the man thing and got an oil change.

MIKE, August 15, 2000

I came to a realization today. Our kids are getting too big, too fast. Sometimes you lose perspective when you are with them everyday. When I took a step back and looked at them, I couldn't believe how big they actually are. I spent a lot of time playing with them today because before you know it, they won't want me around...All in all our kids are great, and we just need to remember to let them be kids while teaching them about responsibility and how to be good people.

KORI, Sept. 20, 2000

I have been writing some books. My idea is to write children's books that are geared toward a father's supporting role in a family. I think this is important because the father has been sort of typecast as the breadwinner and that is it. I would say today fathers are and are becoming more involved in their children's lives; but your daddy is a trendsetter. Your daddy takes you to ballet and swimming and gymnastics...(Writing) has been a very fun diversion. I enjoy writing about families and parent-child love.

MIKE, Sept. 22, 2000

Dropped [Number 1] at school, and did some work at home before heading to [Number 2]'s gym class. There I met a mom of three kids, same ages as our kids, and we started talking. She asked me if I was a stay-at-home dad and, proudly, I said I was. She responded by saying, "I have never met one of you before!" How do I take a comment like that? Am I a novelty? Does she respect me more or less? She said it enthusiastically, so I assume she was impressed? Why does this impress or make it so hard to believe that a dad can be the primary caregiver for his children? She turned out to be very nice and offered to watch [Number 2] while I got [Number 1] from school. We busy parents have each other's backs.

MIKE: One week later I met her husband who was a doctor. His wife was out of town, so he was on "kid duty"—his words. The interaction with him didn't go as well. I felt lots of judgment from him. He said, "How do you do that every day? Doesn't seem very gratifying. Don't you feel guilty not being the breadwinner with a real job?" Now I know why she was so excited to meet an involved father. Guess she doesn't get much help at home because child-rearing isn't very "gratifying," according to her husband.

MIKE, Oct. 2, 2000

After dropping [Number 1] at school, the next two hours were spent upstairs straightening, sorting laundry, making beds, and running downstairs to check on [Number 2] and [Number 3], not sure who made whom cry at that moment. Although it seems like I am complaining, I am merely venting, and not even doing that with an angry tone. I was amazed that I could spend an entire day cleaning and straightening a house.

MIKE, Oct. 13, 2000

Mommy came home from South America this morning after stopping in the office. She was home for the afternoon…

KORI, Oct. 14, 2000

As usual we scrambled out the door to get [Number 1] to ballet on time, [Number 2] an hour later, and [Number 3] gym and swim class somewhere in between. In the afternoon we walked outside on a fall day. We stopped to shop because [Number 1] had chore/commission money burning in her pocket. She bought something for $5 and then wanted something else for $15. When I explained to her that she did not have enough because she spent some money and only had $10 left, she said, "I know, Mommy. I can't hold my horses!"

MIKE, Nov. 2, 2000

After [Number 1] and [Number 2] had class, we went to Einstein Bagels downtown to meet with three other stay-at-home dads. It really felt great to meet these guys. Although I just met them, I felt like I have known them for a long time. We shared stories about how we got started in our "jobs," and they were all very similar. We all felt we were raising our kids well and we made plans to get together again. The annual Stay-At-Home Dad Convention is on the 18th, and we are going to carpool for the event.

MIKE, Nov. 21, 2000

This day wasn't supposed to be so busy, but it ended up that way. The only activity we had was story time, but I think the kids are getting tired of that class; they sit for ten minutes and then run back and cling to me until I peel them off and send them back. At about 4 p.m. Kori told me she could not be home for dinner and had to work late, which meant I had to call in reinforcements because I had a Preschool Board meeting and Choir practice. When Kori finally got home at 11:30, she was chatty but I was done for the night.

MIKE, Dec. 15, 2000

Kori had a vacation day today. [Number 1] had a parent-student party at school this morning, which meant Kori got to go. I usually go, and she normally misses; I let her be the involved parent and I simply observed and watched [Number 2] and [Number 3]. I enjoyed watching Kori and [Number 1] interact while they worked on a craft, but I must admit, I was a tad jealous of her, as that is usually my role.

A year in the life of the family. I wonder what it would be like to do that again, but Mike says no way, not until the next turn of the century.

MIKE: Yes, let's see how long it takes her to figure out that we won't be around then.

Is it normal that I can rattle off the dog's weight, but I stumble to remember the weight of our youngest child?

5

It is humbling to be with a roomful of girlfriends and laugh at the lame things their husbands—fathers to their children—do or don't do, only to realize that you have behaved just like the husband. It is a bit ironic. Shhh! Don't tell Mike. I may have to eat crow for crushing his comparison to our friend Rod, who works outside the home, but who is not as active of a dad as Mike is.

MIKE: I am getting the humble pie ready. Finally I am right. I knew there would come a day; I just thought I would have to wait a few more years.

While Mike gender-identified with Rod as one of the guys, his family role more closely associated with Rod's wife, Sylvia,

who was the stay-at-home parent; and for me it was just the opposite. I listened and laughed as another friend recounted the story of when her husband forgot the diaper bag and had to drive across town to get it, making him really late for an event. Then, in between my laughter, it hit me; I have done that.

On an average week, I routinely grabbed my laptop and briefcase because that was part of my routine, but the diaper bag not so much. When my husband went away for his annual boys' weekend, and I was full-time supermom, I, on occasion, left the house unprepared. It was not every time, but enough times that our oldest child remembers those occasions to this day. Having no shame when it comes to my kids, I would ask another mom for a diaper or a wipe on those occasions when I left baby essentials at home. Believe me, that took some serious skill because I had to first size up the kid to make sure the diaper would fit my child. Our oldest daughter retreated in embarrassment and called me an unfit mom.

MIKE: My, how the mighty have fallen! Remember when Number 1's hair bow for the dance recital was mistakenly packed by the movers the day before the recital? I handled it—running to every craft store in town and learning to make a new bow, but Kori did not let that one go for weeks!

Somehow I wondered what the moms would say if I shared my story. Would they laugh, like they were in reference to their spouses at that moment, or would they laugh and then talk behind my back after I left about how I was an unfit mom for forgetting the essentials every child needs when they leave the house? This is not intended to offend my friends; I might have joined in too.

I might as well keep the true confessions going as a tribute to all the dads or parents who have been laughed at or with for not being a super parent, engaged with every aspect of a child's life. There is just a little twist when expected gender roles are reversed.

Again, my husband, the family manager, was out of town, and Number 4 got sick to the point where I needed to call the pediatrician. As an educated woman with a master's degree no less, I figured nooooo problem. I would call the pediatrician, make the appointment, take him in to see the doctor, and get a prescription. My husband has done this dozens of times with our four kids; I can handle it.

MIKE: This story is about job security for me! In our family, we divided duties so that each of us could focus on our domains. Doctor visits are on my list, and you will see why they stayed on my list.

I found the number, called the office, and got the receptionist who asked for the child's name. Check, I can do that. But the barrage of questions that followed left me feeling inadequate.

Operator: "Pediatrician?"

ME: (Delay...after all, it is a practice of pediatricians.) "I think it starts with a *W*." She reads the names, and I pick one.

Operator: "Weight?"

ME: "Umm, I just took the dog to the vet, and she weighs sixty-five pounds, and he has to be close...I'd say about fifty pounds."

At this point, I can tell from the tone in the operator's voice that she is suspicious of me due to the lack of confidence in my answers. She asks me more questions.

Operator: "Date of last appointment?"

ME: *Oh crap, I don't know that one.* "Umm, a physical in July for school?"

Maybe it was the slight questioning tone in my voice. She continued.

Operator: "Can you tell me the social security number of the primary caregiver?"

ME: *Primary caregiver or insurance policy holder?* "Oh, that's me."

Needless to say, after the Spanish Inquisition from the operator, I got an appointment for him, and today he is all healthy and well, despite his mother's lack of comprehension of the stay-at-home dad duties.

Again, in general—and I stress in general because many health care systems are very concerned, and rightfully so, about patient confidentiality and safety—if a man calls in and can't answer the health-screening questions right away, he is awarded with empathy for being an active father figure. He is forgiven for not knowing all of the pertinent information. After all, he is the dad and not expected to take kids to the doctor, know school pickup times, be able to braid hair, or sew on a button. We women—including me—fall for it every time and run to the rescue.

MIKE: I have to admit I have seen both sides of this one. I have definitely benefited and appreciate the moms that have helped me. On the other hand, my daughter and I have not been included in after-dance class ice cream invites because I am a dad among moms. At one point a mom told me that her husband said it was not appropriate for us to hang out. Hey, I saw the movie *When Harry Met Sally*. I do think men and women can just be friends and nothing more.

And while I am on a roll, I will share one more story to make parents and caregivers feel better about their parenting decisions—laughter encouraged, even at my expense. Admittedly, the elementary after-school pickup scared me—which way to enter the half-moon drive, timing, crossing guards, and the entire bit. I had only seen it in the movies and bought into the hype.

When I had to pick up the kids from school one Friday, I decided to walk. I put the youngest, our preschooler, in the wagon, got the dog, and felt good about doing three things at once—spending time with kids, getting exercise, and walking the dog. I had worked at the office in the morning and made it home just in time to say goodbye to Mike and slip on gym shoes with my work dress. With one hand on the wagon, and one on the dog, I realized that I needed to tie my shoes. In a moment of short-lived wisdom, we will call it, I tied the dog, then a fifty-pound Labradoodle pup, to the wagon so that she would not run away.

Well, she still ran—with Number 4 in the wagon, and she was excited. I ran after her, yelling at the top of my lungs, with one shoe tied and the other flopping and impeding my progress. The toddler, when he realized what was happening, started to scream too. If there had been slow-motion video or iPhones at the time, we might have been another short-lived YouTube sensation posted by a neighbor.

The dog was about to turn off our court onto a bigger street, and I could anticipate, based on her speed, that the wagon would go on two wheels like a racecar. At that point, I am thinking if Number 4 breaks his arm when the wagon tumbles, (a) I know how to call the doctor; (b) he is potty trained so no more diaper bag; and (c) Mike will never leave me alone with our kids again.

MIKE: See, it is all about job security. I never walk up to school; so much easier to drive and manage pickup. I even let the dogs ride along for fun. Everyone wins that way.

Fortunately, the wagon stayed on all four wheels, as did the dog after a few minutes. She finally realized I was calling her name—among my screams—and her racing, front and hind-legs in full motion, came to a stop. I could breathe again, and Number 4 was a bit shaken but otherwise safe. To this day, well over ten years later, Number 4 says, "Remember when, Mom, you strapped the dog to my wagon and then told her to run?"

Well, not quite, but I am humbled all the same.

No, not an illusion; the dog decided this kid should be in the cage. Omaha, 2008.

Number 4 forgave the dog, but Mom still gets the blame for the wagon incident.

Featured in this chapter: Kori   Mike   Number 2

6

This is my fourth oxeye daisy, and I won't stop until the petal I pick ends on "she loves me!"

In every setting—work, home, volunteering—there are always those challenging people who make life interesting. You know the ones who say black when you say white; or the ones who say you do everything wrong and they can do it better; or the ones who just plain, for whatever reason, rub you the wrong way. Team dynamics are part of growing up, but when it comes to the home team, you at least hope that the built-in fan club is intact.

As I mentioned earlier, Mike started staying home full-time just before the birth of child Number 2. I was two weeks over my due date. I was to be induced at 6:00 a.m.; she was born at 2:27 a.m. That's our daughter; no one is going to tell her when or how she will make her entrance—she will decide, and it will be grand.

MIKE: At the risk of getting both of these ladies worked up, I am going to call a time-out. About four months into the pregnancy, my wife found out she was in charge of a big event, scheduled almost two weeks after the due date. I told her that she had enough determination that she would cross her legs until the event was over so that she could be there, and then have the baby. Sure enough, her boss made her take the day off after the event, and that is when our daughter came into the world. Like mother, like daughter.

Due to the circumstances I mentioned earlier, I started working part-time about three weeks after Number 2 was born and back full-time at four weeks. With Mike at home, I pumped enough milk to make sure she got the same amount of breast milk as her sister, even though I wasn't there to deliver it directly. She was a happy baby and got love from the same parents in the same household.

MIKE: Admittedly, I was in a learning curve at home with the two, so that was different for sure. By the way, learning to be a full-time parent is a challenge and not for everyone. My training period with Number 1 involved a lot of daytime help from our sitter, but when Number 2 arrived, I was it for the both of them. It was my time, and some days I had issues getting off the starting block.

Number 2 was not an early talker. As is normal for siblings, her big sister took care of everything for her, including speaking for her when she pointed to something. Looking back, I should have appreciated these moments of silence instead of taking her to get her hearing tested. Alas, when she discovered how her voice worked, she liked it.

Shortly after that was the first time she told me that she did not like me and she loved her daddy. Ouch, that was not just a knife, but also a dagger to the heart. It's like I was a dragon, and she knew the exact vulnerable spot to slay me! I attributed this to all sorts of sophisticated brain synapses involving our new family dynamic of mom-works-and-dad-is-at-home. I imagined that Number 2 told me, "You only stayed home with me for four weeks, so I hate you." And Mike is home all day, giving her kisses and special treatment, and that is why she likes him best. I convinced myself that she knew I took her to the office at three weeks, and, even though I had her black and white flash cards set up to improve focus and eye coordination, she thinks I abandoned her.

Before black and white books were all the rage for baby, I made my own flashcards to help with focus.

MIKE: And now you are meeting the wife I live with every day, the one whose mind races like a hamster wheel at all hours of the day. Many times, we benefit from that wheel running fast; however, there also are a lot of bizarre thoughts that spin through that brain—like our three-week-old knowing she spent an hour in her mom's office. I have asked her, and she does not remember. On top of that, my wife gets mad at me when she asks me what I am thinking sometimes, and I say nothing; literally it is nothing! She is like that hamster running constantly on the wheel, and I am the hamster that digs a hole in the newspapers and takes a nap without any thoughts in my mind.

Yes, I have the capacity to clear my mind and think of nothing. I told her she should try it sometime. She did not respond the way I thought she would. Guess it is better to leave some things unsaid.

Truth be told, I had heard that girls and moms go through this love/hate phase, and maybe, I vaguely remember having some discussions with my own mom. I would have called it reverse psychology. (Why not, when many other things worked differently in our house?) But she was a mere toddler, and while I had no doubt she was and is clever, I did not think that mental manipulation capacity kicked in until later.

At my job I dealt with people who did not like me or rather did not agree with the way I handled something, but I did not give birth to them or breastfeed them, so my expectations were a little different.

I am forever grateful for the counselor who told me this was in fact a phase. My employer had an employee assistance program where I could get free counseling sessions. I had cried all the way to work that day, and yes, sometimes in the bathroom that week, and definitely in the bathroom at home.

MIKE: Yes, I was there. She was inconsolable, and for a while she even held it against me, saying it was not fair that I got the hugs and she got the snubs.

I thought I needed an intervention. The counselor told me this is normal, but I could hear the hesitation in her voice when I told her the age of my daughter. She politely said it was a little early to hear that talk, but it would be okay. She gave me a way to handle it. I needed to reassure her that I loved her, that I was sad she felt that way, and that I would always be there for her. The counselor explained the entire psychology of pushing boundaries and tests, and, of course, in my mind I was laying out a clear PowerPoint presentation to explain the logic of it all. It still hurt.

MIKE: You know how shit rolls downhill. Momma was not happy, so we all had to go to counseling to express our feelings. Uuugghh!

After a number of counseling sessions, I can finally share this story with other moms. I was so ashamed that I had failed on the mom track.

Number 2 is a lovely, talented, smart child that I love very much. Even before she said she did not like me, we butted heads often. In all of our lives, someone serves as our mirror, the person who holds up a reflection of the truth of who we are, the good and the ugly. When I say ugly, I don't mean the wrinkle on my face or the birthmark I wish would go away. I mean those things I do that don't reflect who I am or who I want to be.

This child would be the first one to call me on the carpet when I didn't make it home when I said would. Even if I was five minutes late and made it in time to see her solo in the kindergarten chorus, she would say, "Well, you weren't there at five when I waved to Dad in the audience." When I stayed up all night to make chocolate chip cookies for her class, at her request, because I had to work late to meet a deadline, she would say, "Yes, thank you, but Susie's mom made them and delivered them to school." When I gained a few pounds, more than I had wanted over the holidays, she would be the first to say that an outfit did not look good on me. It was true, so I couldn't chastise her for it, but I didn't want to hear it. She was not rude most of the time, just brutally honest.

MIKE: These two also have been one of my biggest challenges in the twenty years I have been staying at home. My job was often intermediary. If I took sides, I was mean or a bad husband. If I did not take sides, I was unsupportive. This was a no-win.

It became a constant pattern between us. She would keep me accountable for even the littlest detail, showing no mercy. I would try all the bribery—clothes, food, ice cream—and it didn't change. At times I would ask how this elementary school student, who so sweetly hugged her daddy and played with her little brothers, could not only find and magnify every flaw that I had but so cleverly bring me to the brink of despair when she uttered, "I don't like you, Mom."

While I have not heard those words uttered from her lips in a while, I share this story about this letter she wrote, well into her teens. I read a tip from a mom blogger about using a journal to communicate with your children. The idea was to buy a journal for the two of you to share. Write a letter in the journal, leave it on the nightstand of the child or mom/parent, and then wait for the other person to respond. It is a way to express and share feelings in a safe way until the two of you are ready to have a face-to-face conversation about the issues— this was before texting of course.

I will try anything to find new ways to connect to the kids. I realize that all four kids are different, and it seemed that this worked with her. On about day five, I saw a journal on my nightstand and eagerly grabbed it to read it. To this day, I am still amazed at what it said.

To protect Number 2's privacy, I am sharing a high-level summary. I did get her permission to include this story (and she said, "By the way, Mom, that was a long time ago. I know you are my champion"). However, as I continue to build trust, I only captured enough so that you understand the gist of it all.

Mom – I like you. I don't love you, but I like you, and you should be okay with that. It takes me a long time to love someone and for now you should feel good that I like you…

The letter went on to explain her thought process. I was in shock at the message, but also impressed by the clear, logical argument that she articulated. I read it again, and again, and again. I had a choice to make after all of my counseling: (1) I could have a pity party because this child, whom I carried for nine months, loved unconditionally, and praised for being her own person, said she didn't love me; or (2) I could celebrate that she liked me and we had a chance. I chose path two (Remember, this is after a few years of counseling and support from my husband.) and wrote her a note back thanking her, reiterating my love for her, and telling her I would like nothing more than for us to have a mutually loving relationship.

Throughout her early teens, our ups and downs continued. I could tell you many, many sweet moments with this girl and her father, her grandmother, her siblings, the dogs, her friends, and even me on occasion. I also realize that at some point we had four teenagers in the house, and in the words of playwright Oscar Wilde, I was not young enough to know everything, yet I was old enough to know that I know way less.

MIKE: As an only child and boy, my wife says she is amazed at how I handled four kids, two of each gender. I have to say, navigating between the two of these ladies has not been my favorite part of our journey together. Yes, I have been home with my daughter since she was born, and, yes, I have seen her painfully, barely say hi to her mom and run to me. I have seen my wife work really hard at trying to build the bonds, and I also have seen my daughter hurt when she does not get the reaction she wants from her mom. There are the days when I say, "Put me in, coach. I will go to work outside the home." It can't be harder than dealing with these two.

If I was at work, and intervening between two employees who had conflict, I would have to admit that I have not been totally innocent in provoking the conflict. We definitely know each other's vulnerable spots and can pull those out too easily. Number 2 is a very talented singer and entertainer, and my singing, at times, is like nails on a chalkboard to her. Like a kid, it makes me sing louder some times. Every once in a while, I like the house to be in total order, including no clothes on the ground, and she tells me, "You can just shut the door to my room," but the mound is so large, I can't even shut the door.

She has a number of strengths as an independent thinker and worker, and she has a lot of compassion for others (maybe not for her mom). She is and will be a great leader. I know she loves me—she has on a few memorable occasions said that—and she knows I am her champion.

I like to think she is a closet member of my fan club. You know, the people who pretend they really don't like someone or don't care, but are secretly following their moves. She actually took my advice the other day, but then Number 1 said, "Mom, don't make a big deal about it. You will blow it." I just drew a daisy on a piece of paper and put it in her room, making sure there were only enough petals to land on the phrase, "She loves me!"

Comments from the Peanut Gallery:
The Voice of Child Number 2

One of my favorite photos of Number 2 and me, an intimate moment captured on camera. 2002

Number 2 in playful DIVA mode; love it! 2011

Everyone has that one person whom they just know how to annoy or get a response from. For me that person is my mom. You see, she just made it too easy for me. My intention was never to hurt her feelings. It was just something I would do when I was bored because I knew she would react.

Now that I have moved out of the house, I do really miss the playful banter. Both my parents claim that my mom and I are so alike, and that is why we would constantly fight over small, petty things. Of course, I would perpetually deny that fact because I refused to believe that I was like her. To this day I couldn't tell you why I didn't/don't want to be like my mom.

But now I am learning how to live on my own across the country. I am learning that I am very similar yet oh-so-different from my mother. We both, definitely, are our own people, and we embrace the shit out of that, but, as confident as we are—or seem to be, one stupid comment from some irrelevant person can still tear us down from the inside out.

I'm sure my mom really wants me to talk about how, when I was a child, I told her she was the devil, or when I told her that I just don't really like her that much. Well, guess what, Mom, I am not! And no, I am not just doing this to push your buttons, but I am sure that it did a little. But, honestly, I would like to think that the things I said back when I could hardly eat my own food would not determine what my relationship with my mother would be for the remainder of my life.

Mom knows, even if she doesn't like it, that I don't like talking about much. In my eyes, it's kind of my own business, and if someone tries to pry into my life and ask me a ton of questions, it usually leads me to getting more closed off. My mother, Kori, loves to talk, ask questions, and probe at me until she gets some sort of answer that seems satisfactory to her.

As I have really started living on my own, I find myself doing the same things my mom did that annoyed the hell out of me; for example, whenever my roommates or friends go off and do something fun, I make them tell me their top three things of their day or of their trip. Also, when my roommates are having trouble, I'm usually the person leading the conversation and finding a way to deal with the conflict at hand. SUCK THAT, MOM. YEAH, I AM DEALING WITH CONFLICT!!!!!

But honestly, I see myself doing the things that probably annoy my siblings and me the most when Mom does them.

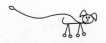

Whenever we would rant about something, and we were annoyed, she would always talk about what the other side was thinking. And let me tell you, I didn't give a rat's ass what the other side was thinking. I just wanted her to stick up for me and my side, but she would always persist in trying to force me to see the other side of the story. And now I'm doing the exact same thing with my friends, and I don't even notice until I'm in the middle of it.

Long story short, being like my mom is not a bad thing. Actually, she is an amazing woman, and I am proud to be her daughter. But I'll never tell her that because she will cry, and I can't deal with that, and then she will want to hug me, and I don't do hugs—but that's a whole other story.

You might want to check with your YouTube mom to make sure it is okay

7

In reference to the African proverb, "It takes a village to raise a child," I am in total agreement. I'm sure when that gem of advice was first uttered, the village elders did not even envision YouTube or reality TV, which became legendary teachers in our house—fortunately, for good. Even into her twenties, however, Number 1 still feels the need to tell me that she first will consult her YouTube mom for advice.

It started out of necessity. I was leading a Fortune 500 corporate foundation at the time, and to execute the strategy I created, it required a lot of travel to various sites across the country. For the most part, these were one- or two-night trips at max, and it made logistics much easier with Mike at home with the kids.

MIKE: Easier for her, of course. She got to sleep in nice hotels with clean sheets, dine out, and talk with adults while I, well, let's just say mornings could be chaos getting four kids ready for school—two with long hair that needed more than just a brush-through, and two that chased each other around the house, not wanting to get dressed at all.

We moved the family for this job, and, at the time, Number 1 started fifth grade. She was being a trooper about the move, for the most part, after she got her pet and the first family dog (now one of three dogs). But still, she had anxiety about new friends, a new school, new teams for soccer, and more. As a mom, even though her dad was at home, I felt tremendously guilty on the days I saw her struggle, and often went out of my way when I was at home to help her transition—hence the dog. I had moved as a kid about every four years, and I knew what it was like to start at a new school.

Great addition to the family, 2006.

Number 1 vying for yet another puppy.
Aren't three dogs enough? 2016.

About a month into the new school year, I had a trip to California, which with travel meant I was away for about three days. Just after I left, she called me and asked how to French braid hair. All the girls were doing it at school, and the next day her new group of friends were all going to wear French braids. I am now hundreds of miles away; family members are hundreds of miles away; and I don't know my neighbors well enough yet to ask a favor.

MIKE: I could do a mean ponytail or pigtails, and I could even put bows in the hair, but that was the extent of my hair ability. I told Number 1 I would help her, but she wanted mom on this one.

Then I remembered something that happened at the office. A younger colleague showed me costumes she made for her and her husband to wear to a party. When I asked how she learned how to sew, she told me all about YouTube (note it was still fairly new when this happened) and how they have instructional videos for everything. Eureka!

I told Number 1 the story about my colleague and told her to look for a video on YouTube about French braiding hair. She called me later that day; she did it and was proud of it. Crisis averted, and my husband's ponytails still worked for Number 2, at least until I got home.

I should have known that was just the beginning. There is a point when your preteens and teens just need mom. Even though her dad had no problem buying tampons, and would even FaceTime her from that aisle at the grocery store to make

sure he got the right ones, Dad did not know how to tie ribbons a certain way; he wasn't into the latest fashion craze; and he didn't know how to apply makeup—neither do I all that well, for that matter. Each time I was away, and I didn't know how to help her, I encouraged her to consult YouTube and would even send her a cool video I saw about new hairdos or cutting T-shirts certain ways to bring an old shirt a new stylish look.

It got to the point where she would, on her own, share tips with me that she learned from YouTube, and I have to say that she is far better than I am at hair, makeup, and a number of other things in life that she has naturally picked up with ease. The first time she said, voluntarily, that she would go "consult her YouTube mom," while I was standing right there, I was a little taken aback. I mean, I was right there—next to her. Granted, I did not know how to help with what she asked—some sort of new eyeliner technique—but I at least wanted to be asked.

MIKE: Oh! This mother-daughter thing; it's killing me. I mean she did not ask me, and I am with her all day, but that did not bother me. Okay, it did not bother me until she got older and went to her mom for advice first. I mean I was with her all day—through cuts and bruises, the tampons, worries, temper tantrums, and hugs.

As YouTube mom continued to be a household phrase into her late teens and early twenties, she came to me one day and said, "Mom, you should be really excited about something—a milestone moment for you as a parent to celebrate." I got so excited, wondering what it could be. Would this late teen, almost twenty-year-old child of mine be giving me a compliment? Will she be removing YouTube mom from her vocabulary and finally recognize all those times I rocked her to sleep, consoled her when friends were mean, listened when a school day went badly, picked her up from soccer, and stayed up late to help her do her homework?

Instead, she said, "Mom, in seven months, I will be twenty. Even if I got pregnant today, I will not be a teen mom, and you should be really happy about that. Congratulations."

Again, I was a little stunned; it was not what I expected to hear. It was something to celebrate for sure, and it was a nod to her favorite reality television show about teen moms.

Truth be told, the National Bureau of Economic Research said the MTV show *16 and Pregnant*—one of her favorites—ultimately led to a 5.7 percent reduction in teen birth in the eighteen months after its television premiere, accounting for about a third of the overall decline in teen births in the United States. MTV's show did not do it alone, but it was a contributing factor.

Eyebrows on fleek (Did I say that correctly?) 2016

Natural beauty in and out. Family adventure out west, 2010

And so it goes; YouTube mom still has a room at the house. MTV is part of the village now, and although we limit its visits, it still has a spot at the table. We did celebrate a milestone birthday when Number 1 not only looked and felt great, but could never be a teenage mom.

MIKE: Amen.

Who taught him bleep, bleep, bleep, donut hole, bleep, bleep?

The forbidden fruit of the young family of four kids (two girls and two boys, all a total of six years apart): guns, swear words, and the television show *SpongeBob SquarePants*. Why the latter? Well, there were so many shows on television that the kids asked to watch that Mike and I, in a rage to cut back television-watching time, finally had had it when it came to a sponge wearing square pants. It could just as easily have been a ball in round pants or a triangle in an A-line skirt. We'd just had enough.

MIKE: I think she might be using the proverbial "we" here. I like a little noise in the background, and if it had been ESPN or CNN that she protested to, I would have said slow down now.

For whatever reason, the banning of *SpongeBob* worked when they were younger. When they went to the houses of other kids, who were allowed to watch the show, Mike or I got a call from the parent reporting that our child told them they could not watch it. Now, in term of guns and swear words over the years, those were like the serpent himself sliding along with our children, saying, "Just do it; grab that stick, and pretend it is a gun." or "You are in middle school now; you should be able to say what you want—your friends are doing it." Like Eve, they got roped in, and like Adam, they blamed a sibling or someone else when they got caught, and even threw Dad under the bus: "Dad saw us, and he didn't say anything."

MIKE: Why am I the bad guy here? I am around kids all day. My wife is in a work environment where people drop the F-bomb, and I can tell when she is around those people a lot when she recounts a work story to me.

Let's start with the guns. I had been adamant, even before the kids were born, about no guns in the house. I have been around many responsible gun owners with safes in the home, and they also hunt, and I respect that. I was more worried about the kids thinking guns are play toys, not the serious weapons they are. Despite the children—in particular, the boys—begging for Nerf guns, we stood our ground.

MIKE: I was raised this way too, no guns in the house, but truth be told, I loved going to play with friends who had toy guns. We played good guys/bad guys all the time. I don't own any real guns today, and I turned out okay—I think.

We had been successful for years; however, I noticed the boys made guns out of anything—from sticks to rulers to French fries and more. An experienced mom who had an older son asked me how I wanted the boys to react if they found a real gun in the park. She said the likelihood of a boy picking it up, when it had been forbidden, is much higher. She said to think about the option of letting the boys have the toys, but also talk about the rules and responsibility of toys, weapons, and violence.

It made sense, and now our boys own enough Nerf guns to outfit the entire neighborhood for pretend battles. So far, we have not had to confiscate any as a result of a Nerf bullet hitting someone in the face or a private part, which was rule number one for responsible Nerf gun ownership at our house. Rule number two is putting them away; somehow, we have stepped on a few and even found Nerf bullets in our bed.

MIKE: I have enjoyed a few house Nerf wars in the past few years with the boys. We invite the girls, but they have little interest in these games we find to be fun and entertaining.

Now, to address an issue that every parent faces when children learn the forbidden words—or, as 1980s comedian George Carlin refers to them, the seven dirty words you can't say on TV. There was a time when our young children also stayed away from the "D word," as in dumb. I had convinced them that it was not a word we use in the house because I really just don't like it.

When one tattled on the other, saying, "She used the D word," we had to riffle through our mental dictionary to remind ourselves what a D word was to a five-year-old. Today, the D word has taken on new meaning, and often my teen boys like to show me a list of 175 ways to refer to the penis—one being dick. It provides endless hours of laughter for all three boys, husband included.

MIKE: Come on. You can't take the boy out of the guy, even as a parent. Now that it is just the boys and me, minus two young adult sisters, we laugh a lot at "dumb" stuff. I did have to counsel Number 3 when he took it a bit too far. Kori, now outnumbered these days as the girls have gone to college and beyond, asked Number 3 to put the toilet seat down. Our comedian quickly said, "No, Mom, since you are the only girl now, you have to put the seat up." We are working on comedic timing and appropriateness, but you had to give it to him on that one. I laughed my ass off!

We certainly are not prudes and have on occasion dropped one or more of the seven words, but it is just not a practice I admire on a regular basis. I tell our children it is a lazy use of language to whip out one of many swear words in a situation, and I give points to those who actually creatively use the English language to describe behavior, rather than boiling it down to one word for effect.

We all know, however, that for children the forbidden words can be very enticing. I will never forget the face of our youngest when he realized he was allowed to say "HELL" during the Apostles' Creed that we recited in church. He would get so excited at that point in church, squeeze my hand, and shout it out as he looked up at me with an expression that said "I am doing something you would normally yell at me for, but you can't say a darn thing because it is in the Bible and we are in church."

Now, my sister, who is a wonderful aunt to our four children and our brother's kids, would treat her nieces and nephews to all sorts of indulgences that qualified as okay during aunt time—the time when the kids could get away with some things that normally Mom and Dad did not allow, and it could range from ice cream and candy before bed to, well, the swearing game. The irony is that I would not even associate a swearing game with my sister.

Here is how the game works. When the kids were riding with their aunt in the car, she set a timer for three minutes, and during that three minutes, the kids could say whatever they wanted without penalty. Had they asked me and explained the rules ahead of time, I, of course, would have said no, but that is the glory and fun part about being on aunt time. I had no idea about this game until the six of us—Mom, Dad, and four kids—were in the car the next time on a road trip, and

the kids begged to play the swearing game. I called my sister to get an explanation, and she started to laugh. All she said was let them play once and call her back after the youngest child does his thing.

MIKE: How bad could this be? They are home with me most of the day or at school, and I know what they watch and who they hang out with. This will be a dull few minutes.

We thought about it and after success with the guns-in-the-house experiment, our hope now for the swearing game was that if the kids could say it for three minutes in a contained space that they would get it out of their systems. We agreed to allow the four kids ranging from thirteen to seven to have three minutes of no-consequence, free-language time. We both naively thought, *What could come out of such innocence?* Were we ever in for a surprise; Mike and I exchanged looks of utter disbelief to laughter to bewilderment, and blamed each other for where they heard such things.

My sister was right. While all the kids had their moments, our youngest, Number 4, strew together the longest potty mouth connectivity of the seven words and beyond, and somewhere in between he threw in the words *donut hole*—that is all I can repeat here. I kept watching the clock, wanting the three minutes to end, and it seemed like time stopped among four little potty mouths, each trying to outdo one another and each putting together enough words to make my husband and me understand that these kids had way more exposure than we had anticipated.

MIKE: Again, I maintain to this day that I hang with kids and dogs all day, so I am not teaching them that shit. Kori continued to refer to me as Adam from the Bible when God said why did you eat the fruit and he said, Eve made me do it. I have to admit I was laughing so hard that I almost had to pull the car over! My face hurt for a good ten minutes after they had finished with their game. I knew I would be playing this game again with the kids, with or without Kori.

I am not sure when children Number 2 and Number 4 went to construction worker or trucker school, and I mean no disrespect to truckers or construction workers. We know many lovely people who work in these professions. Maybe they secretly found George Carlin's skit on YouTube (Was it even available then? Surely we did not allow them to go on there.) when Mike was not monitoring them at home.

MIKE: Easy now. No need to blame this one on me.

We no longer play the swearing game in the car, as they all feel they are old enough to say what they want, and for the most part are very respectful. On occasion one slips and sometimes we let it go. Sometimes we tell the kids to aspire higher and use better language, and sometimes there is a grave consequence if it is in front of an inappropriate audience, like the young next-door neighbors who may be

playing the swearing game soon and the parents will look for scapegoats like us.

The good news is that we have never, in public, and friends can attest to this too, heard our youngest child, Number 4, or his siblings for that matter, say or call anyone a BLEEP, BLEEP, BLEEP, BLEEP, BLEEP, BLEEP, BLEEP Donut Hole, and for that we can rest at ease. His potty mouth has at least been contained.

Comments from the Peanut Gallery: The Voice of Child Number 4

Number 4 stylin' in his tap costume at the National Dance Convention, 2012

Going to the high school winter dance, 2016

My sisters and brother think I am the most spoiled, but in a few years, I will be the only one at home, and I already am frightened about what my parents will do. They go to the extremes from telling me they will leave me meals for the week while they travel, to telling me they look forward to when they can give me all their attention at once. I will take the first scenario, please.

My parents always put me on the spot, asking whom I want to take me to my dance team competition—hip hop, tap, etc.—and when I hesitate, Mom reassures me that I am not going to hurt her feelings if I pick my dad. She is always worried about our feelings. You want to know what is going through my head? Mom buys me more stuff, but Dad lets me have pop whenever I want, which will be better for me that weekend.

The family calls me the baby, and I asked Mom about that because I am in my teens, but she said I always would be known as the baby, like she was and is in her family. When they are home, my big sisters do take care of me, but I have other not-so-fun things that come along with being the youngest, like when people boss me around, including Mom. She likes to drink TAB soda pop and she makes me go get it for her like I work for her. When I say no, she says that she gave birth to me and that my head was really big, so I should be nice to her. At first I did not know what that meant, and now I just say, "Gross, Mom, I have heard that one."

Sometimes, even now, when I ask Mom to pick me up, my brother shows up. Inevitably, Mom gave him a few bucks for us to get a drink or snack on the way home, but, come on, she picked my sisters and brother up when they were younger, and I know this because I often had to ride in the car with her to get them.

Dad told me that, when I was younger, I said I wanted to be a photographer or stay-at-home dad when I grew up. Now I am thinking something else. If I do have kids one day, I do want to be like my dad. He's there. He's funny.

He supports me. Even though he makes a really funny Chef
Pierre character in the kitchen, I still think I will take cooking
lessons so that I can make more than casseroles.

Mom hangry for homework, kids hating hunger challenge

9

As a self-professed—and then StrengthsFinder® validated—lifelong learner, I read, listen to, and attend presentations as much as I can about everything from self-improvement and team effectiveness to work-life integration and family management. I take a lot of notes and come up with at least three action items to do or change as a result of the learning.

MIKE: This is another one of those work traits that I could pass over. Why do we always have to make things better? Isn't it okay just to be okay for a while? No, because she made me take the StrengthsFinder® too, and mine is harmony. Yes, I like it all to work smoothly, while she wants to change things all the time. This is not harmonious! Guess who always ends up losing the argument to make it harmonious once again.

At an executive women's work lunch a few years ago, I remember a professional woman talking about the importance of intentionally sharing the good work stories with your kids, especially girls, so that they learn to appreciate that work is a rewarding and gratifying experience. It was a light bulb moment for me as my kids had just come off a career day, and I asked if they wanted me to speak the next year.

After all, my job leading a corporate foundation meant I got to decide how a large company invested millions of dollars in various communities across the country. I traveled to a number of places, met with some of the leading experts in the country on food insecurity, and got to partner with talented people, including celebrities, on occasion, that supported the cause.

My kids, however, when I was at home, only saw me on my computer and phone and knew that the job took me away from them, sometimes on birthdays or over weekends. I often had to take a call during a soccer match and may have missed them score a goal. They told me "No way" did they want me to speak at career day because my job was boring; all I did was email and call all the time. I had to change my ways.

After driving the kids all over town for soccer matches every weekend for years, all we got was this AWESOME photo.

MIKE: I ended up videotaping a lot, even when she was there, in case she got a call at a crucial moment. This was so we could also share the moments with out-of-state family too.

I made it a point to share what I did on business trips. I not only communicated the challenges, but the good things too, like the heroes I met who helped feed children that did not have access to meals during the summer. I shared video clips of when I was on *Good Morning America* to make a donation on behalf of the company. I talked about the fun of meeting one of my idols, a professor who not only did prize-winning research on underprivileged women, but also was a great advocate who taught women to find and use their voices to become activists themselves. Years after I first heard her recount authentic stories of people who overcame obstacles to support families, I had the privilege to be on a panel with her.

I told them stories about travels to India and meeting school children who did not wear shoes, ate lunch on the dirt, but loved seeing the pictures I took of them with my phone. Our kids could not believe these kids had not seen pictures of themselves when their every moment was documented in film and then digital files. I brought them to volunteer events, and only once had an issue with Number 4, who wanted a gift bag and threw a fit when I told him he could not have one as he was a volunteer. (I made up for that. A few years later he learned to ice skate with former Olympic medalist Nancy Kerrigan who was at an event the company sponsored.)

MIKE: Yes, I had to carry the crying child out of the building and sit in the car with him when the clients of the nonprofit asked why my wife was yelling at him, not knowing she was his mom and he was throwing a fit about not getting a fuzzy blue pencil.

On family vacations, I also got a kick out of hearing the kids ask why we were watching that man say the same thing over and over again when my wife decided to use a little car time to edit work videos. She said it would be a good break from the kids watching a movie to see her CEO speak about other events, and she could edit at the same time. That leg of the car trip was a long one.

Then I decided to engage the entire family in the national food stamp challenge, an exercise for people to empathize with what it is like to live on about $5/a day (per person). At the time, my job was to promote the company's signature cause of child hunger. I worked as a Vice President of Cause Integration and directed the foundation under the company's name. The kids and I co-wrote a blog post that is on the website of the national nonprofit, Feeding America, about our seven-day challenge.

Start of the #SNAPChallenge
by Kori Reed of ConAgra Foods

Kori Reed, wife and mom of four children—three teens and one preteen—also is vice president, Cause & Foundation at ConAgra Foods. She champions the company's signature cause of child hunger. She and her family are doing the food stamp challenge for the week, Sept. 15–Sept. 21. This blog is co-written by Kori and her kids.

From the Kids:

- My mom doesn't understand. My chubbly—name for stomach—is still hungry. I like pizza, and a lot of it; and one peanut butter sandwich is not going to be enough for me, especially after school. She doesn't know how hungry we are after school.—age 14

- WHAT? Can I use my own money to go buy an ICEE? It is a drink, not food. Why does my mom make us do these things? What do you mean we don't have enough money to buy cheese crackers this week?—age 11

- Mom really didn't ask us to do this. I am worried because my siblings are going to eat everything today and we will run out of food by the end of the week. My brother ate almost all the grapes today at lunch. I went to the store with mom to look at prices.—age 17

- This is dumb! I don't need to do this to have empathy for someone else. We can't have ice cream this week. Fine, can I have butter noodles?—age 15

From Mom:

As I responded to each child's comments, I held my smile, but on the inside realized I was facing one of my worst fears, not having enough food for them to eat. In the days after 9-11, when we all worried about what might happen next, I was the mom that put peanut butter, baby formula and water under the bed. I couldn't handle the thought of eight eyes looking at me saying we are hungry, and not being able to do anything about it.

Fast-forward, I am fortunate I get to do the job I do, and I am fortunate that the SNAP challenge is a seven-day exercise for our family. I can handle the temporary crankiness among the kids; however for millions of families, in particular single parents, it can be months or years of worries and wait related to food. This is why we are doing the challenge, to give the kids a new perspective on food, a basic element we take for granted every day; and for me to not lose sight of a cause I touch every day.

MIKE: I am proud of my wife for the work she has done. This was a pretty eye-opening experience for our family, putting a strict budget together, managing meals, and telling the kids they could not have what they were used to getting at the store for the week. What I realized is that parents will feed their kids first, and that is what we did, which meant no leftovers and often no second helpings for me, even when the first portion was pretty small with four teenagers in the house.

I am not suggesting that the kids became advocates overnight, but I can say we have made progress. When I first started in the role, and our son wanted yet another video game, I told Number 3 that some kids just want an orange for Christmas, and he asked me if that was a new personal gaming device. After I explained what fruit is, he then said he would share his game and bring an orange. You can't blame the kid for trying. That one keeps me on my toes, which is why I need to continue the lifelong learning so that I can stay one step ahead of him.

Please, Mom, no more... 2011

Featured in this chapter:

Kori

Mike

The new battle of the sexes: Balancing men's and women's suffrage in a house where the bitch rules the roost

There is something about a house of three females and three males that makes discussions lively. Not that the sides of an argument are divided by gender, but our house is loud and at times full of animated discussion on topics that include feminism, gender roles, and physical challenges on strength. It would not be unusual for daughter Number 1 to challenge son Number 3 to an arm-wrestling match after he says boys are stronger than girls, and then it would start all over again when she says girls rule and boys drool.

We do have three dogs in the house too, a female Labradoodle, a male Cockapoo, and a female Bichonpoo—all great family members that I often wish could share their thoughts on goings on around the house. The Labradoodle, dog Number 1 and family member Number 7, is a senior citizen in dog years. She is wise beyond her years, a matriarch, protector of the house and her peeps, and master of her domain; and while Mike is the alpha dog, she likes to walk me a few times a week.

Mama Bear, Papa Bear, and Baby Bear out for a walk.

MIKE: I trained that dog and all our dogs from the minute we got them. I walked around the house with carabiner clips and leashes attached to my belt loop from the time they were pups. I tried to explain to my wife the concept of pack animals and needing a leader, but she did not want to follow the rules. She said she had to manage people all day at work and she did not want to do that with the dogs. She let them eat when they wanted and sleep on the bed. Of course, our Labradoodle walks her.

I have to be careful playing the gender card as Mike and I are raising young people, two of each gender, and we have the duty and honor to help them be the best people they can be. The two genders are made and process information differently, as John Gray points out in the book *Men Are from Mars, Women Are from Venus.* In true confession form, however, I have cracked a few jokes about the difference in the way a male mind works, something about "GL-ing" things, a code I use for Guy Logic.

MIKE: I know that was her code for no logic, and she said to me often, "Quit 'GL-ing things." It may not be logical to her, but to me, it's all good.

The genders are different, but there also are some cold, hard truths that point to the advantages of a particular sex: (1) the glass ceiling does exist, and we know this is true by the gender inequality in corporate boardrooms across the country (females are far underrepresented at 20 percent in 2015, according to Catalyst, an organization dedicated to expanding women's opportunities in business); (2) women are underrepresented not only in the boardroom, but also in higher-ranking leadership positions in organizations; and (3) it is a fact that overall women are paid less than men. These are facts.

There also are studies that show some overall differences in how men and women get work done. Men create relationships and do business outside of the boardroom (on the golf course, at business dinners, or on business trips) and build informal networks. According to another study, about half of women surveyed name "exclusion from informal networks" (old boys' network) as the main factor holding them back in their careers. In general, women get credit for being more detail-oriented, but when they ask questions and probe based on that detailed knowledge, they get labeled as assertive or demanding—or a bitch. I have worked with male colleagues who champion their female counterparts and some who are…well, less aware.

MIKE: This is where our daytime role reversal gets interesting in that we can relate to many couples, just sometimes the opposite gender spouse. When I worked in marketing, I spent and looked forward to a lot of time on the golf course. I also have prepared my wife with talking points covering Sunday night football when she had to board a plane with her male colleagues on Monday morning.

For women in the workplace, gender expectations and inequality can be confusing. Research shows that women make positive impacts in the workplace; however, actual treatment in the work setting does not reflect that research findings. While I have done all right and reached the vice-president level, over close to twenty-five years in large corporations, I have been underpaid for my job level—namely early in my career (validated by HR records), winked at in a boardroom, called fatso by another manager when he knew I was pregnant, accused of having an affair with a vice president when I was younger, and the list goes on—too many to count.

One day, after a $3 million negotiation I managed hit a snag, I got frustrated when the organization with which I was negotiating went above my head to a male president. It was within the right of the organization to do that, but we just had a lot of room to go before enacting the escalation process. The male president, without hearing my side, asked if I wanted to be known as tough and demanding.

The reality is, I think he thought he was sincerely trying to help me. I said I appreciated his advice, and I wished that he had seen me in action to actually point out when I was being demanding—what specifically I was doing at the moment—so that I could learn. I said my intent was to be a good steward of the company's money. I am not above feedback. I have been in the room when many men and others whom I admire negotiated multi-million-dollar agreements, and I'd say I was tame in comparison.

MIKE: My wife is a good debater and will stand her ground. I have yet to see her be disrespectful in a professional discussion with others, unless she is with me and maybe I will admit to not listening to her a few times in a row. In general, however, before we have a "discussion," she has thought through every argument and can have a response to my objections.

I shared the story with the entire family that night at dinner, and it was interesting to hear the reaction from the kids. Our daughters consistently have called me a feminist, and in their sarcasm, I could tell at the time it was not a positive reference. Even though I had hoped to serve as a role model, at that point in life, in their early teens, the girls told me that they did not want to be like me. They wanted to be stay-at-home moms and be there for their kids.

While that stung at the time, I said, "Great, just be the best you can be at whatever you decide." Of course, as many young people who search for independence and decide whom to be, their sentiments have wavered over time. I highly admire parents who chose to stay home, obviously. Whatever they decide in life, it should be the best situation for them and their respective families.

> MIKE: And at some point, both our boys said they wanted to be stay-at-home dads when they grew up; today they are not sure, and it changes. That is okay too.

As a mother of girls and boys, I told them at dinner that night that I champion for both genders. I explained that a feminist is someone who believes in social, political, and economic equality of the sexes, so this is an issue for men and women, girls and boys. I am grateful for the advocates who have come before us like Susan B. Anthony and Gloria Steinem who were dissatisfied with the status quo and marched for change. I reminded them of their history lessons including the nineteenth amendment, ratified in 1920, which gave women the right to vote (their great grandma was born in 1918). I also tell them the facts that women still, to this day, do not have equal pay as compared to men. That last point always gets them—a simple measure of equality and money, and they asked an innocent, "Why not?"

MIKE: I have always, since we were sixteen, admired my wife's passion to advocate for issues. Sometimes that passion is not leveraged to my advantage. Every once in a while she craves a good debate. Like any marriage, we accept the entire package. I have read the facts and I may not be as vocal as my wife, but I hope my action as the stay-at-home parent has shown our kids that there are a number of ways to succeed.

Much to my appreciation and delight, the boys agreed with the girls that it was not fair that men and women did not have equal pay. I avoided my high horse lecture about society, equality, Rosie the Riveter, Title 9, and so on. I told them they had a chance to change that and that they might want to study about equal pay more and see what actions can be taken. I literally saw my husband let out a breath he had been holding in anticipation of a giant lecture about women's rights, which to be honest would not have been out of the norm.

MIKE: She got that right.

Then we as a family had a really interesting conversation about societal expectations and gender roles, ranging from the way people treat male nurses and female race car drivers to the way Dad is treated as a full-time parent—a man among moms!

By now I hope it is clear that the title of this section, "the bitch that rules the roost" refers to our Labradoodle. Oh, I have been called a bitch in my time, not on the home front—at least I don't think so (let me know if you see anything on social media from our kids), but at work for sure. I am in alignment with a blog I read on the topic that describes a heartless bitch as working hard for what you want and knowing when to stand up for what you want, not in an arrogant or self-promoting way.

Our female dog knows what she likes when she sticks her head out the window of the car. She sits in the backseat by the car window, knowing she wants me to roll it down so that the speed of the vehicle makes the wind plaster her hair back on her face. She is regal, not arrogant or demanding. She is not taunting the male dog to join her. She is enjoying her time with her fellow "friend"—and that is me!

Our first dog, family member
Number 7, rules the roost.

"Mom, are you really the lawn authority?" | 11

Imitation is the biggest form of flattery, until it is used against you, and then flattery becomes, well, infuriating. Meet child Number 3.

In the never-ending quest to become better parents, Mike and I took a class called Parenting with Love and Logic, based on a best-selling book written under that title by Foster Cline and Jim Fay. Truth be told, we took it more than once, maybe three times, and, yes, most likely because Number 3, our first boy, came into this world just when we were getting comfortable as parents, and God decided to give this one a little extra attitude.

In his toddler years, he had two modes: run and sleep. I sincerely appreciate the mom who told me not to worry—this was normal for a boy. As a child he was sweet, compassionate, *and* a comedic snake charmer at the same time. He bares an impish grin when he thinks; and while he is a stereotypical third-child peacemaker, we never know what is going to come out of his mouth. At age seven, he started massaging my shoulders and, due to fatigue, my guard was down; I came to just in time to hear him say, "Mom, I was thinking I needed a new pair of shoes."

When he was even younger, we had to take a year off swimming lessons, at the instructor's request, because he liked to jump in the water and laugh, even when it was not his turn. At church, during the children's lesson, the two dads and the pastors had to practically tackle Number 3 and his friend who both decided it would be fun to chase each other around the front of the church while the rest of the children sat to hear the lesson. We had him tested for attention deficit and any other nerve-related issues. The answer was no; he was just all boy to the extreme of the stereotype.

MIKE: In the early days, when all four were under six, I had to always make sure he was in the grocery cart first, and I had visions of that scene in the movie when a terror of a kid runs all over the store, and you hear over the loud speaker, "Clean up on aisle nine!" With him, I might have been able to convince Kori that using a backpack leash was justified.

Even at age five, he reminded me of some colleagues I worked with who were really smart, but I was not sure how they would use those smarts, so I had to be really clear about deliverables. Number 3 loved the sociable side of school, but not the work. At age five he needed to practice writing his name. Yes, maybe like the lines on the paper for Number 1's scissor skills exercise, but he was five.

One night after dinner, I told him he could not leave the table until he wrote his full name—spelling out his first and last given names. I could tell he was thinking, and it was potentially not good when I saw the impish smile and dimples come across his face. He looked at me, picked up the pencil, and wrote his two-letter nickname that we do call him all the time. I am convinced he knew full well that I meant his entire six-letter first name and last name, but I did not specify. Round ten to him!

MIKE: They all have their moments. With him, I have to remind him to use his smarts for good and not evil. Again, I was with all four of them all day and night when she traveled and stayed at luxurious hotels and talked with real adults. I had to keep a sharp mind to these master manipulators who could mask their real goals with a sweet hug and a kiss. Who had it worse?

The principles of parenting with love and logic are all about natural consequences for actions. It is about helping the child understand that choices have outcomes, some good and some bad, and if it is bad, what are you going to do next time? If you don't do a chore that is expected, you don't get allowance. If you made the choice not to do your homework, and you know good grades are expected of you, you don't get to go to the after-school activity.

If a child is upset, let him be upset and reassure him by saying, "I know you are upset right now, but I know you can handle it"—even if it means you lie down on the floor at Walmart with him and whisper it in his ear as he is having a full-on arm-and-leg-kicking fit.

MIKE: Ask Kori what the natural consequence is for being late for dinner or not showing up where you are supposed to be, when you are supposed to be somewhere. She could do it for a work flight or meeting, but somehow not for dinner. When she showed up an hour early for an event because I purposely told her the wrong time, I said "I know you are upset right now, but I know you can handle it." She learned a valuable lesson. When I ask her to be on time, there were not-so-natural but well-fabricated consequences when she had a history of not showing up on time for family events. For her it was having to wait an hour for a band concert to start when I told her an hour early, and she chose to listen that one time. At least we got great seats out of the deal.

From the day these kids are born, they grow increasingly independent from us, and our job is to foster that. As adults we have consequences for actions—some that we don't like at all—but from an accountability standpoint, the outcome is based on choices that we make. We can't control all, of course, so I am referring only to those choices we can control, like leaving work on time rather than addressing one more email before running out the door.

Over the years, we had varying levels of success with consequences, when we did not let our emotions get the best of us. When two of the siblings were not getting along and they came to us for the third time, we had them sit in time-out together and hold hands. When the emotions got the best of us, after hearing the same whining from the same children, we put ourselves in time-out.

MIKE: We learned the parent time-out too late in life. After all these years of starting with a calm voice, then escalating, then yelling after sibling arguments did not stop—and after we confirmed there was no blood—we should have done the parent time-outs in our own room.

As the kids entered the teenage years, we picked up more sage advice from parents who passed before us. Mike is way better than I am at picking his battles, and he introduced the phrase, "I love you too much to argue with you." In essence this means, "I am no longer going to fight with you; just do what I asked." This is a popular one in the teenage phase.

While Mike is a problem solver, as most men/dads are, I am okay if the kids make their own decisions as long as it will not harm them or become a safety risk. Number 1 sometimes is overwhelmed with too many choices, and I know if I decide for her, then I'm the scapegoat if she is not happy with the outcome. I offer my opinion and often follow with "This is not a life or death decision; you can handle it."

MIKE: Okay, mind you, I love Number 1 and 2 and 3 and 4 and would do anything for them. Number 1 sometimes has stress over which jeans to buy. As a guy who hates to shop, I would just say, "Yeah, looks good; let's go." Number 2 would never

> care what I thought. Number 3 doesn't even wear jeans, and Number 4 would want to know if they are cool looking enough for him, as if I know.

This is not to say we always acted with love and logic. We have made our share of mistakes; however, the kids have heard these phrases enough times to know we are serious.

Back to Number 3 and consequences—it is his job to cut the grass each week, and he decided to put it off. It was not a life or death situation. We were annoyed, but it did not have to be done that day.

> MIKE: She says that now, but she was the one tugging my arm to nudge him, especially when the toddlers next door thought visiting our yard was a trip to the jungle when the grass went over their knees. I apologized to the neighbors and asked for patience as we taught our son about the consequences of the delay.

Finally, he got out to the garage, and, already in a foul mood, it got worse when Mike told him he had to cut it twice and bag it. It was the lesson we had been hoping for—the natural consequence of the delay. As he cut the grass, we could tell he was frustrated with the length of the grass as it made the work a little more difficult and took longer. My husband and I were about to high-five each other, thinking our patience had paid off.

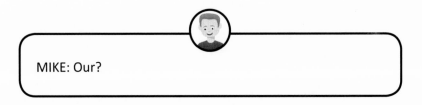

MIKE: Our?

He was glistening with sweat and he was frowning, and we thought, *Lesson learned.*

Lest we ever think we have outsmarted this one. Mike had to run Number 4 across town, and when I looked out the window again, this time in the backyard, I noticed Number 3 was not bagging the back lawn for a second time as he was asked to do.

He said, "Mom, I made the executive decision—it did not need to be done."

I applaud the leadership, but any good leader also needs to know when to follow. To make matters worse, when I started to argue with him, he said with his sweet, boyish grin, "Mom, I love you too much to argue with you."

The key with this kid is that he is not a rude smart ass. He has mastered the tone of slightly poking fun, and he does it in such a way, with good comedic timing and appropriate context that it almost takes you off-balance, and you want to laugh. I tell him that he should use his brain for good and not evil. If you remember, this is not the first time this statement has been used on him.

In relation to the lawn, I should have known what I was up against. I gathered my composure, and after a back-and-forth debate, he said, "Mom, are you really the lawn authority?"

MIKE: I am glad I was not there for that one. Not that she needed my help with him anyway. I would have blown a gasket on that one. All that love and logic would be out the window. He is her mini-me in her younger years, but in a male body— socially smart with a touch of sarcasm and a smile to win you over. Glad she handled it.

Again, I am observing his leadership authority—I have seen this behavior at work—and at the same time thinking this skill of his could be put to good use some day, but not today. I replied, "Because I am your parent and I asked you to do so, you will do it"—something my dad said to me when I was his age.

And it all comes back together in the circle of life, or at least generations—imitation, sometimes flattering, and sometimes just darn infuriating.

Comments from the Peanut Gallery:
The Voice of Child Number 3

Crazy hair, crazy kid, and we love him all the same. Fishing, 2007.

Number 3 and his grins, always making us wonder what he is up to next. 2016

Mom is making me write this, but in return she agreed to buy me the snack I want, and I declined to cut the grass for another hour until she met my demands. She might forget later, and she knows it. That's the way we roll, Mom and me. I asked her if I could write that Mom is a beacon of hope for this family, until she gets mad and grouchy, but she said that was not enough to justify her trip to the store to buy my snack. I had to write more.

Usually for her, a hug from her teenage son is worth a few bucks for a snack after school, and if I say no to going to dinner with her and hold off just long enough, not to the point where she is mad and going to threaten taking my phone away, but just long enough, I can get some more bucks out of her. I get that she wants to spend time with me, and I get the value of that. After all, there is value in time. Time is money. I have to go to dinner with her and actually talk with her, and she is so intense, always trying to get me to share my feelings. I love her, but her questions are draining.

So let's talk about Dad. My dad is probably the best dad in the world, except when we don't like his dinner casserole or he is on the sidelines of one of my sporting events.

Let's talk about the casseroles. When Dad does not have dinner planned, you know it is going to be some kind of noodle casserole all mashed together. Sometimes it can be casserole three nights in a row, and this one night it was beef and corn mixed. None of us liked it, and I was the one to tell him that. He gave me this look on his face that I hate, with his lips smashed together and the wrinkles on his forehead were clearly showing and he raised his eyebrows.

When it comes to sports, Dad is at every one of our events, except when he has to drive Number 4 somewhere. And don't get me started on Number 4, who always needs more time and energy from Mom and Dad, and they give it to him. I always do better when Mom and Dad are not there. Dad is on the sidelines yelling things like "get in the post," "you are center," or "get in ready position." One time at my sister's basketball game, the ref stopped by our seats to tell Dad it was only an eighth-grade basketball game and the world was not going to end. How embarrassing!

Mom had a different approach. Knowing Dad's sports temper bothered me, she would only say good things, like "good job," "keep shooting," or "you will hit it next time." But after the game I turned on my phone to see a bunch of texts, saying "good job honey, next time when you are running up the court, you might want to try this," or "follow through on your shot," or "we may want to practice that reverse layup a bit more."

All in all, the fam is cool, and don't tell my sisters I said this, but I miss them. My parents still won't let me convert my sister's room to a man cave, although I keep trying, and I have a really good plan for it. This might take a while—maybe more hugs or dinners with Mom or eating more of Dad's beef-corn meals with a smile.

12

Is a boy calling his mom sexy a normal part of development? The keys to repressing Freud's Oedipus complex

Before anyone gets too "weirded out" by the teachings of Freud, the boys are doing just fine today, and as you have seen in other stories, they have made it through Freud's phases. Today, they are in that phase of life when they think that their dad is a "cool-but-sometimes-embarrassing" dude. For some reason I, on the other hand, according to them, don't know anything about sports, despite being invited to be a walk-on as a college athlete—that I did not take—and they laugh when I suggest to them how to enhance their batting stance or play defense on the court.

MIKE: You have to give me something, Kor—with my boys— my tribe, as you say.

As a late-forty-something working woman with four kids, sexy did not make the top of my priority list.

MIKE: It did for me.

Sure, it crossed my mind when I was with my husband, but at that time in life, those sexy moments were few and far between—falling somewhere between soccer and basketball games, dance recitals and college visits, business trips and looming corporate-related deadlines.

There are different forms of sexy. In my favorite *People* magazine, I skim pictures of people in awesome physical shape, wearing high fashion, and doing glamorous things. There, sexy is in a 32C bust and 26-inch waist supported by toned, tall legs that look way awesome in a bikini. That is not the way I roll.

MIKE: Well that is not my definition of sexy. My wife is sexier than any of those models in her trashy magazines.

What I find sexy, attractive, and interesting is the confidence that actors like Steve Martin, Lily Tomlin, Morgan Freeman, Pierce Brosnan (in his later years), and Meryl Streep exude. The wisdom and quiet confidence in their own success allows them to play unique characters and makes them, well, sexy. The kids know these are my favorite actors and make fun of my choices. They also often have been unwilling, yet captive audiences, joining me while the actors are on screen.

After all the talk over the years about wisdom, success, and sexy, I should not have been surprised when child Number 4 asked me what made me *successexy* one day.

MIKE: Good one, Number 4. I was not at dinner that night. I am sorry I missed it. All the dinners I have cooked and cleaned up afterward, and he chose the night I am not home to say something that I am sure I would have laughed hard at.

I think I was a little retro-shocked because I had gone through something similar with his older brother, but with a different twist. When Number 3 was six years old, he told people he thought his mom was sexy. We are not sure where this came from. While my husband and I, admittedly, got more relaxed with Number 3, we did not go around the house calling each other sexy—at least not in the kitchen or in our son's living space.

As soon as we all laughed (big mistake), it became a permanent part of his vocabulary, and he pulled it out often. Now we laugh about that, but at the time, I thought, *Oh, my gosh, what do the neighbors think?* When his little brother asked me about successexy, my memories of panic resurfaced.

It started with the questions game. At meal times—when we had them together—from the time the kids were all little, I asked them questions, including the following: What are the three best things that happened to you today? What do you want to be when you grow up? If you could choose to have any superpower, what would it be? And so on. I wanted the kids to learn how to engage in conversation and know that their answers mattered, and that we as parents were here to listen and learn.

MIKE: My wife is known for asking questions, and she will keep asking them as if there is a blue ribbon for question-asking, her own little contest, but she also remembers the answers, and that is annoying. She remembers everything.

By engaging our kids in dialogue, I was avoiding one of my biggest fears that was acted out in a PSA (public service announcement) commercial: The fifteen-second spot showed a dad reading the newspaper, while the son ate his cereal. After ten seconds of no conversation, the character-generated headline said, "Missed opportunity to talk with your child about drugs." Whether it was sex or drugs or rock 'n' roll, I wanted the kids to be able to converse and appreciate dialogue as a way to get to know themselves and one another.

MIKE: This is one thing that my family, when I was growing up, would not think about doing—having detailed conversations about a variety of topics, even the taboo ones. I had a big learning curve on this when I joined her family and we started our own family as well. My brain doesn't think like hers. When she asked our boys about their progress on puberty, I had to remind her that it was my job to have those conversations with them—and away from the kitchen table. I am so glad now, however, because these conversations have added so many good memories over the years. Hopefully our kids will carry on the tradition when they start their own families.

Over the years the kids may have gotten a little less interested in talking to me, especially as teenagers. During that time I was accused of being a too-involved parent and told that most parents drove the car in silence and did not barrage the passengers and friends with questions. I told the kids that I cared about them and their friends and wanted to know them better, but they said, "Care a little less."

On the other hand, my husband, who is much less inquisitive but no less interested, did pick up a lot of gems when he listened to the kids talk in the car. I do think it is fascinating that to this day, including when I was a teen, kids don't realize that there is no soundproof window between the driver's seat and passenger seat. Having a party at the house can be a real learning experience when we are picking up the soda cans or making sure the bonfire is still going strong.

MIKE: Yes, my wife used to get really mad when I got more scoop than she did about what was happening in teen world. I told her it's less about talking and more about listening—the kids don't even realize you are there. She insisted on asking questions and engaging them in conversation. Sometimes, you just can't change a person's ways.

Child Number 4, when he was still a sweet, non-teen who was just shy of turning ten years old, still liked to play the question game, or at least he humored me. During one night of Mom Q-and-A, I asked each of the kids to ask a question of the people at the table. Number 4 asked me, "Mom, what makes you successexy?"

After a few seconds of silence, as our brains processed the word for a minute, we all burst into laughter. It was the type of laughter that made tears of joy roll down your face, partly because you needed a moment to process the "new" word, and partly because it was so shocking out of the mouth of a child—a surreal moment for sure.

It is not that sexy is a bad word; it's just not something I wanted to hear from our maybe-not-so-innocent elementary school kid. After we all laughed, he explained that he "messed up," and that he blended the two words. He really meant to ask me what makes me successful (which, by the way, was a great question).

MIKE: He is the youngest of four kids after all; we did have to threaten the older ones that if they spilled the beans on Santa before he was ready, they wouldn't be enjoying Christmas Day very much.

The irony is that I really appreciated his effort. When he was in kindergarten, one of the first pictures he brought home from school included two stick figures and the text said, "I like dad. I love mom." Before you say "Awe, isn't that cute," the next month he drew a picture with three stick figures with names above them: "me…my dad…and my teacher," all holding hands with the teacher in between the two. I was not even in the picture. The next three months produced pictures with these sayings: "My dad and me going swimming"; "I like to play with my dad"; and yes, there were more.

11-12-07
I liKe DaD
I lVœ MOM
DaD MOM

That is so sweet!

me 8-28-07 Mrs. H. Dad

*Wait, now I am not
even in the picture?*

10-3-07
I smile
I P I i woh
like + play with my
d A d

*FINE, play with
your dad! :)*

9-21-07
My dad
and me going
swimming
DAD

I don't even rate on the drawing scale?

MIKE: Well, he was with me all the time. This is one advantage of being a stay-at-home parent. I got the hugs and the pictures, but I was also dealing with homework, picky eaters, snotty noses, and laundry, while she was on a plane, eating out, and spending time with other adults. I was running the family business.

By the way, it was only a picture from the eyes of a six-year-old. I never held hands with his teacher—although I did joke to Kori that I didn't mind being her room parent. And, in contrast to the "I like dad, and love mom picture," I also got one of my most memorable moments with him when he said, "Dad, I am having a great day and 50 percent of it is because of you." I did not need to know about the other 50 percent. Kori would have asked.

The blend of the two words also took me down memory lane to one of my absolute favorite TV shows when I was a kid, *The Electric Company*, a 1970's educational show associated with the Sesame Workshop. The show targeted elementary school children who graduated from *Sesame Street* and were working on developing grammar and reading skills. Accordingly, the show featured a segment where two cast members appeared in silhouette, one uttering the initial sound of a word (*th*) and the other the rest of the word (*ing*); then, the two pronounced the entire word in unison, *thing*.

Perhaps it was the fond memory, and the thought of, "You say *success*, and I say *sexy*, and together we say *successexy*," that made me laugh. I guess I should have been really happy. It could have been *success* and *less*, *absent* and *mom*, or *complete* and *failure*. That would have been a real bummer and put sexy into far better perspective.

This is how we roll. Omaha, 2014

Featured in this chapter:

Kori

Mike

There are moments in life when we wish we could reverse time and take back the one thing we said that triggered a series of unfortunate events. This was my year, and I triggered it by my sarcasm. In our family, we call them God Winks moments, when He needs a little humor and says "Okay, you want to play it that way; let's see how you handle this one."

At the time, my career was going well. I was wearing two hats, maybe three at the time: running the corporate foundation, working on cause marketing for consumer engagement, and chairing a national organization called the Association of Corporate Contribution Professionals. I was certainly busy, consistently on a plane for the majority of the month to speak at conferences, attend board meetings, or explore potential new partnerships via a site visit. I had hit a groove.

MIKE: At that time the kids attended three different schools—elementary, junior, and high school. We were still in not-in-a-groove mode, and I was trying to just stay above water.

It was a rare weeknight at home when at least four of us were at the T-ball field for Number 4's game; there is nothing better than a summer night, with munchkins smiling on a T-ball field, half of them into the game and the other half dreaming of the snack after the game. It was his friend's birthday that night, so the treats were extra special. We knew the birthday boy and his family, and we had a lot in common; his mom worked outside the home, and his father was a full-time, stay-at home dad to the two boys.

I noticed his wife was missing, and when I asked, I learned that she was on a business trip and would arrive back home by 7:30. Her husband said she was feeling terribly guilty.

I reached out to her and did only what another working mom who travels a lot can do—gave her a hard time. It was all in jest and with great empathy, but definitely a fine line only someone "in the tribe" can cross. You know those "in-tribe moments" when only someone who is of the same gender, race, nationality, or experience can acceptably make a joke about that gender, race, nationality, or experience. Anyone outside the tribe makes a comment at high-risk of being racist, sexist, and/or rude.

MIKE: I think I am in my wife's tribe, although at times I am not sure. We have grown up together since we were sixteen, so sometimes she tells me I have crossed the line and that she is not one of the guys—she has feelings. What does that mean?

The intent of the conversation with my friend was to say "thinking about you," in a way that did not make her cry while recognizing her personal and professional emotional challenge. She said she would be home that night, was just hoping her plane was going to make it back on time so that they could have a late dinner. I wished her well, said I would give her son an extra birthday wish for her, and that we would catch up later.

Well, I spoke too soon. While my job at the time required a lot of travel, I had yet to miss a special family occasion. That night, however, after gently teasing my friend, it was as if the floodgates opened; the karma fairy and God winked all at the same time. Not two weeks after my moment of "razzing" a friend, I found out that I would be absent for my youngest child's actual birthday, and gone the day before and the day after; I would not be home in time for dinner for three days. I would not be home at all for Number 4's special day. YIKES! I reached out to my friend, told her my story, and apologized, saying "I learned my lesson, and I spoke way too soon." We both laughed, in the way only someone "in the club" can do to comfort you.

MIKE: She laughed with her friend "in the club," but I got the tears and the anger. Maybe I am not in her tribe. I then had to do everything she likes to do for birthdays in addition to all those things I do for birthdays. I had to do double-duty.

As parents of four children, we have to balance equitable and fair all the time. Do we spend X amount on presents for each kid at holidays or do we make sure each has the same amount of gifts? If one child gets a treat at the store, do all four get a treat at the store? If one child chooses to stay home from a shopping adventure, and those of us who went decided to go get ice cream, do we have to bring that child ice cream home?

What most parents experience is that kids can't count how many times you had to yell at them to make their beds or pick up after themselves, but they have an innate sense to know and keep track of the times when Number 1 got X, but Number 3 did not; or Number 4 got Y, but the other three did not. It is crazy.

MIKE: Yes, and for the most part, this is my territory. She only has to face it full-time on weekends. While she travels, I am 24/7, and I give a high-five to any single parent out there. I love my kids; some days, I wouldn't mind a hotel room, a long shower, and silence.

To this day, Number 1 holds a grudge because Number 2 happened to have a birthday dinner with Shamu at SeaWorld. While that seems really big, and maybe even fair for her to feel jilted, we were at a family member's destination wedding in Orlando, and the wedding was on Number 2's birthday. In order to make her feel special, and not get lost among the wedding excitement, we arranged for her own celebration cake when the entire family got to have dinner with Shamu. We still laugh at the picture we have of Number 2 getting her cake in the foreground of the photo, while in the background Number 1 is glaring, and she, to this day, proudly claims it is a look of "What about me and my special moment?"

And it continues into the teen years. I realize I am making the kids sound like spoiled children, and for the most part they are, but we have been blessed that, so far, they have made good choices on the big stuff that matters.

MIKE: Amen.

After realizing I was going to miss Number 4's birthday that year, I decided then and there I would do the most fair and equitable thing: I would be out of town for all family birthdays that year, including being apart for my husband's day too.

MIKE: Does mine count? I was on a mission trip with the youth from the church.

At the rescheduled family birthday celebration, after I returned from my trip, and after Number 4 opened his gifts, I announced to the family my plan that I would be traveling on business for each child's special day. Once again, it was as if putting that thought out in the universe made things happen. My job required enough travel that I did not have to make up excuses to be gone. I legitimately had business travel on the birthdays of the other kids. I convinced the family that this was a good thing because it extended the birthday celebration well beyond the actual date. There would be two celebrations, one on the actual date and then one when I returned.

Once again, I am lucky to have a spouse/life partner/ husband, who will help me carry out these schemes and pick up the pieces.

MIKE: You've got that right. You can keep saying that too. I don't hear it enough.

I did need his help to continue a tradition that I started when the kids were little. I got the idea from a working dad of five children. His family custom involved bringing the kids breakfast in bed on their birthdays. It was just something between dad and child, and a special bonding time the kids came to expect. He recounted, from his perspective, the day of their birth and told them special stories about their childhood. I eagerly asked him if I could pick up his tradition and implement it in my family, and he said of course; he had gotten it from another dad.

Well, on this year of being gone for equity purposes, Mike helped me carry on the tradition. On the actual day of the child's birthday, he would bring breakfast in the room and hand the kids the phone and then exit the room to allow us to have our time.

It wasn't quite the same as the live event, but it helped us carry on our mom-kid ritual that the kids still like today; although as teens they may take a bite of the pancake or a sip of juice and then ask me to leave as I start to recount the story of their birth. At this point, Number 3 offers to skip his birth story, so that I don't get near his bed. He loves his bed and is fiercely protective of his space. As a side note, I am fortunate, I guess, that my husband does not like breakfast. He would rather sleep, and I can't, obviously, tell him his birth story.

MIKE: Let me set the record straight on this birthday breakfast thing. Yes, the kids like it and, even at eighteen, announce on birthday eve what they want for breakfast in bed. That is a good thing. However, as the kids got older, a twist was added. I would get tapped on the shoulder around six a.m. as she jumped in the shower, asking me to make pancakes so that she can deliver them when she is ready. When did her tradition become my tradition? Why did I have to wake up early? I had all day to make a cake! Ha! Ha! Guess I am part of her tradition.

We made the best of the situation. I could not go back in time to change what I said, but now I know that one child could not complain about it—actually they all did in unison. To this day, when they want to get to me, they will ask if I am going to miss their birthdays again this year. I just smile, see the forest through the trees, and think, oh look how they are bonding over a shared experience.

Family peace, 2006

Family conflict: Sister gets dinner with Shamu. Number 2 pouting in the background somewhere. Orlando 2005

14

When my life flashed before my eyes on the big screen, it looked a lot more glamorous with Sarah Jessica Parker in the working-mom role

Most people in the movie theater laughed at the scene, but I experienced flashbacks that were powerful and real. I lived it, and it was no laughing matter at the time. I got the dreaded call from my husband that our kids had lice, and I was about to board a plane to take me to one of those mini-pivotal— meaning it was a big step toward a bigger step—career meetings in Washington, DC.

The movie is the 2011 *I Don't Know How She Does It* starring Sarah Jessica Parker (SJP) as Kate, a character who likes her job as an investment banker and loves being a wife and mom. If you haven't seen the movie, I highly recommend it. I think of it as Carrie Bradshaw from *Sex and the City*, a character SJP brought to fame in a successful HBO series and two movies, meets suburban working woman. Even if you are not an SJP fan like I am, any working woman can relate to the struggles her character portrays in this movie, balancing a successful career and prioritizing marriage and family. She tries to be a superwoman, but in the end confesses to the stay-at-home moms—who are characterized somewhat as her nemeses due to the perfect picture they set—that she bought her bake sale pie from the market down the street.

I can relate to so many scenes in this movie, with the exception of a size 0–2 frame on SJP and the handsome boss, Pierce Brosnan. While I am no SJP, I have yet to meet a boss who hits on you for your brainpower, ideas, and work ethic; and when you politely tell him he doesn't hold a candle to your husband, he still respects you enough to promote you, and you continue working together. I am sure he was modeled after a true character in investment banking. I am just saying, in my twenty-plus years in corporate, I have not met any Pierce Brosnans or Jacks, as was the name of his character.

MIKE: Good to know. I love my wife's mind and the entire package, and I don't want to compete with people who don't wear spit-up worthy clothes or cargo shorts for extra storage. On any day, I might find Kleenex,® asthma inhalers, extra medicine, money, and maybe a pair of extra socks in those pockets. My wife does not like cargo shorts, but they are my equivalent of her big weekend purse, so she puts up with them.

In one scene in the movie, as Kate arrives at a potentially career-changing meeting with Jack, she gets a text from her husband that the kids have lice. Immediately she starts itching and the funny scene ensues, with her attempting to mask the itching while delivering a serious proposal to her boss. The movie varies a bit from my experience in that, when she returns home, she and her friend go to a "lice" spa, where beauticians are combing through their long hair while they talk away. Who knows, maybe they have those in New York, and it did make for a better movie scene than what I did.

MIKE: She talks about how it affected her in DC, but says nothing about the endless hair combings and treatments I had to do with the kids at home, not to mention being the dad who took the kids for haircuts only to have the stylist announce in front of a full waiting room that our child had lice and couldn't cut her hair because of it!

For days I had to comb through four heads of hair, twice a day—some long, some curly—wash sheets, bedding, and more. I would rather that memory not return. I wish I was the one in DC, and she was the one doing all the lice removal.

I got the text when I arrived at the airport, after a full day in the office, heading to a trip to DC for a key meeting with a partner. As I ran through the presentation I had prepared, practicing for the next day, I get the text message from Mike that all four kids had lice. I panicked!

All the way to DC I did not rest my head on the seat. Thank goodness for wireless airplane access. I looked up the symptoms, careful not to show the screen to the person next to me. I went to the airplane restroom and picked through my hair like a monkey picks through the hair of his young. When I arrived, I paid the taxi driver extra to stop by the only open pharmacy, bought a lice kit, and spent the next few hours in the hotel applying that as well as ordering a side of mayonnaise from room service. I read that mayo kills lice. I thought *If I do the lice kit and the mayonnaise treatment, surely I will kill those buggers!*

As it turns out, the meeting went fine, and I did not have lice. That was one of the only times I was sad that it was only a one-day meeting. I did not want to go home after this trip. Mike sent me pictures of all four kids in shower caps, looking a little sad. After day two, he threatened to cut all their hair off, as combing through thick hair section by section, four times, twice a day was getting the best of him.

MIKE: What did she do when she got home late? Said she had to go to work the next day, so she would sleep on the couch and be gone early in the morning. Hmmmm. I was on to her. That night I had to go "meet the guys", so she was on comb duty. She tried to protest, but I was onto her game. Truthfully I had done all the work at that point and just wanted her to be part of the process and feel my pain a little.

Once you live through it, it is not so bad. I mean don't get me wrong, I don't want lice again, and one child had it twice, so we have had our fill. We lived through it, and they made a movie scene about it. Okay, maybe it was not based on our story, but we know we are not alone, someone else had to experience it to spark the story. In the end, families are connected by similar experiences—we are more similar than different.

Ah, the days of mayonnaise hair "masks." To this day, Number 1 can't even look at a shower cap the same. Number 3 continued to call them lice caps for some years. 2009

Instead of carving my pumpkin that year, I made it a tribute to household colds, runny noses and lice. 2009

Featured in
this chapter:

Kori

Mike

Number 1

Number 3

15

The night I paid $2,000 to spend a little quality time with a couple of the kids; and why I will pause the next time I am offered a "free" hot dog

The hot dog is one of the most talked about, controversial, and phallic foods, which is part of a mainstream diet from the time a person is toddler age to the ripe old golden days. It can be part of an everyday meal or a special occasion picnic that brings families together.

Throughout a person's lifetime, hot dog topics include (1) what is in it; (2) the health effects of eating them; (3) toppings of ketchup or mustard and relish; (4) and who can forget all the quotes about the hot dog as a wiener? I live in a house with three males—one "adult" by age only, and two teens. Wieners are so much a part of our dialogue; well, that is for another story.

MIKE: In the infamous words of my wife, "Dat true." The actual phrase is "true dat"—but that is my wife, always putting things in her own language. That is how she rolls, and the kids like making fun of her for it.

My mom was never a fan of hot dogs, so I didn't eat a lot of them as a child, but occasionally, I really do enjoy the dog, especially a Chicago-style one with celery salt and a poppy seed bun. It's not something I would make for a meal, but at the ballpark or at a picnic, that's when I get the craving.

MIKE: Come on, how many meals does she make? Yes, the kids and I like hot dogs, and mac and cheese, and beans and chili, and more. We just eat them when she is away.

When faced with the decision between a store-bought, flat, preformed burger patty or a hot dog, I will pick the latter and did at an all-employee lunch meeting. I had not eaten a hot dog in a while. Little did I know how that decision would play a big role in the events that unfolded later that day, leading to perilous teen driving, a trip to the emergency room, and quality time with two kids who got to know me a lot better—more than they wanted.

Driving home after work that day, I felt pain in my stomach, right shoulder, and left arm. It was that kind of uncomfortable pain that you hoped would go away after an intense, deep stretch. I was constantly shifting in my car seat, and I am convinced that the person driving behind me must have thought I was dancing to the beat of the music as my head extended forward to arch my back, and then with my hands on the steering wheel, I rolled back in the seat to relieve the pain in my lower stomach. I thought I would be okay if I just could make it home.

I got out of the car, shouted hello to my family, and ran straight to the bathroom, yelling that as soon as I got out, I wanted hugs all around. Again, I thought I would relieve myself and release the pressure, but it did not work. I sat for a minute, and at that point, only the three dogs were excited to see me.

Two of our kids were not home. The oldest, then fifteen, and our third child, then twelve, sat on the couch watching TV. I barely got an audible hello from the two who were engrossed in a movie. I was kind of relieved because, at that point, the pain was getting worse, and I didn't think I could handle a hug. My husband, who was concerned (thank you), met me at the door, took one look at the pained expression on my face, and instantly knew that something was wrong. I explained my symptoms to him, and he took immediate steps to call the doctor.

MIKE: Again, I am going to step lightly here and may plead the fifth going forward on this one. She usually handles pain much better than most in the family, so when I saw the look on her face, I knew this was not an ordinary, run-of-the-mill pain. Also, having known my wife for a very long time, when she is determined to handle something her own way, she does not use the best listening skills, and I become the target of her denial and frustration and anger. I'm not going to lie—I live to avoid that!

I resisted going to the doctor at first. It was a Friday night so my only choice was urgent care or the ER, and we had not yet met our annual deductible. I also thought I was tough enough to wait it out. I gave birth to four children naturally—no epidurals for me. I can handle pain. I rarely go to the doctor. The only time I go is when I absolutely have to: for a cough that just won't go away without prescribed medication, for a mandatory physical for work, or for a serious symptom that is a sign of something more serious. That just doesn't happen to me, or so I thought. (P.S., Learn from me, and don't live this way. Your doctor is your friend.)

Mike was scheduled to volunteer at a mandatory parent-volunteer shift related to one of our kids' activities, and he suggested switching shifts with someone to take care of me. Through my pain, I shouted, "NOOOO!" After all, we had to volunteer, and I reminded him it was really the only night we could due to our schedule. If he didn't volunteer that shift, we would be blackballed as the parents who don't volunteer, the ones who are not active on the team, the ones everyone sneers at when they show up for the fun stuff, but not for the work shifts. For the sake of our family's reputation, I could tough it out. If it got worse, Number 1 could drive me to the emergency room. She had her driver's permit.

As we waited for the nurse to return the call, he left the phone with me, gave instructions to the kids, and said he'd check in every fifteen minutes. Finally, he was out the door.

MIKE: Just to be clear here, I am the more nurturing parent when it comes to physical injuries and illnesses, and the entire family knows it. She is the emotionally supporting one, and I am the go-to guy for cuts and bruises and the like. It was hard for me to leave. Kori will say, "No blood, no temp, go to school."

Aside from her delivering babies, I have been to the doctor way more than she has; however, as the stay-at-home parent who would be seeing these parents at other kid events, I did not want to be labeled the no-show. It did not take much convincing for me to go volunteer, and if her condition was serious, I had a valid excuse to leave early.

Not more than ten minutes later, the nurse called. I described my symptoms, intense pain in the upper portion of my abdomen, and back pain between my shoulder blades, specifically in my right shoulder. She asked my pain level on a scale of one to ten, and I qualified my response first by saying that I have a high tolerance for pain, having given birth to four children without an epidural; I said I was at about a seven.

When I told her I ate a hot dog earlier in the day, she said that was the culprit. She explained that fatty pork can be a trigger for a potential gallbladder issue and that she could not diagnose me over the phone. The only way to know for sure was to run some tests at the hospital. It was already 7:00 p.m. on a Friday night. She said that I had a couple options, including going to the emergency room or waiting to see if the pain went away.

Before I could even decide for myself, Number 1 put it in perspective, "Mom, would you think about your children for a minute? We need you to be around and well. I am driving you to the ER."

Wow, that was a low blow, but hats off to her for masterfully playing the guilt card. I knew I was raising a smart one, but this was beyond clever, even strategic and results-oriented. Yes, I went.

MIKE: I have to admit that over the years I have used guilt to get the kids to do what I wanted, as I was trained as a child in the same way. There is a point though, when the kids display a master influence skill you marvel at as a parent. This is one of those. My wife would not listen to my advice, but Number 1 knew the right buttons to push. Well played. Looking back now, I can say it is a good trait, but not when they use it on me. That's taking it too far.

Most fifteen-year-olds are excited at the chance to drive, but not Number 1 at the time. Even if I wasn't feeling well, she would have preferred that I take the wheel, but I was in no condition to drive, so she accepted her duty. Number 3, who was twelve years old, did not want to be left alone and went along for the ride with his handheld game unit by his side.

Number 1 drove extremely slowly in the right lane at the pace of a new, nervous driver. On any other day, I might have been annoyed, wanting to just get there; but that day,

I appreciated it. The bumps were less bumpy, the turns were smooth, and I could take pride in multitasking—always thinking of the daily to-do list—getting our daughter to drive while also taking care of myself.

Number 1 takes one for the team on this one. Mom loves pics!

MIKE: Good thing she was distracted at the time. Number 1 was a really new driver, and even I did not want to practice with her.

When we arrived at the ER, I was thankful that it was not crowded—not as much for me at the moment, but for my daughter's ability to park. She found a spot far enough away from anyone else, and then her nerves got the best of her, and she turned the car off. When I got out of the car, I saw that she had made it between the lines, but the rear end was hanging between the two rows. I smiled and thanked God that it wasn't crowded. We could laugh about that parking job later.

We registered, and I was given a hospital armband. At that point, Number 3 looked up from his DS game, and it clicked: Mom was at the hospital. When they called me to an exam room, all three of us went and met the nurse. Number 3 continued to play the DS when the nurse asked me a battery of questions about my diet, eating habits, and pain. Once again, I proudly shared my story that I had given natural childbirth to four kids.

MIKE: She wears that fact like a medal of honor. I couldn't wait any longer to mention it. She really likes to tell doctors this, like they are gonna really care, but she is convinced it is a barometer for pain tolerance. I know I am proud of her for it! But let that not fool you. Behind that tough exterior is a compassionate, kind person. I know where the soft spots are in her armor. And she doesn't get a cough often, but when she does, well, that is another story. I have to wait on her hand and foot.

I knew pain, and I was in pain. The nurse touched my abdomen and took my temp and blood pressure. When she left the room, Number 3 said he was uncomfortable being there and hearing this personal and intimate information about me and my body parts. It was funny because at that time his voice was changing, so he said in a deep man tone, with an innocent boy face, "Mom, I don't want to hear about your body." I told him he could go to the waiting room and play his DS there. He would not move a muscle.

At that point, the doctor came in, asked me a few more questions, touched a few more spots, and ordered some tests. He then asked about my pain. Feeling the need to justify my hospital visit, I started with the usual natural childbirth story, adding that I had to take Pitocin with the last two, which intensified the labor pains. Of course, he knew what Pitocin was, but I needed him to know that I was not one to go to the doctor for minor aches and pains.

MIKE: This is a work hazard for her. Always feeling the need to explain or justify the "business" case of why and how...we are used to it by now.

After the doctor left the room, Number 1 asked me why I needed to tell everyone about the natural childbirth, and she mocked me by reciting it verbatim. I explained to her that a number of people go to the emergency room, sometimes for minor aches and pains, and I wanted them to believe that this wasn't just a bump or a bruise. I knew what real pain was, and this was it! Come on! Wouldn't anyone believe me?

Apparently, I couldn't even convince the medical equipment. I went from an ultrasound unit to a machine that first required me to drink this nasty liquid, which made me feel like I peed my pants and tasted like I licked a metal pole. They found nothing. My husband arrived just in time to hear the diagnosis. The doctor, who I believe was not convinced from the start that I had anything wrong, gave me paperwork that, in essence, said here's my phone number if something happens again. Instead of his phone number though, it was the number of my actual doctor. It was as if he was saying, next time, call someone who cares or believes you.

(Okay, in fairness to him, he had not been there when I delivered our children—even the two boys with 90th percentile head circumferences, so he did not know my pain tolerance.)

Perhaps it was a gallbladder attack or a silent gallstone, or maybe not. Truth be told, at that point, the pain had subsided, not all the way, but it was less intense than it had been in hours. Perhaps all of the activity of the day had distracted me, or perhaps "something" had passed that relieved the pressure that had been causing the pain.

Dressed and ready to go, the jokes and teasing started before we even left my hospital room. Number 1 recounted to Mike her imitation of me talking about natural childbirth. Number 3 told him how uncomfortable it was to hear about mom's bowel movements and see them touch me. At that point, his tension left and his humorous side came out. He imitated me and the nurse and the doctor, replaying everything he had witnessed, all told through the eyes of a twelve-year-old boy. We all laughed.

As we turned the corner, a woman came running after us with a determination to catch and stop us. I thought that I had left something on the bed or in the room, and I stopped to talk with her. The words out of her mouth shot another pain up my spine, and this time it was not physical—it was all in my mind.

She said, "Ms. Reed, how are you going to pay?"

It was the ER billing clerk, and she was already after me to put a down payment on the services for the day. Wow, that was fast! I appreciate efficiency, but this was amazingly fastidious; on the other hand, not something I expected. Mike pushed me ahead with the kids, and he stayed to handle that, thank goodness.

At the end of the day, my free hot dog was most likely the culprit that triggered the pains that led to a $2,000 hospital bill. On the positive side, our family met the medical insurance deductible early in the year. It took away the sting of that first-of-the-year injury or doubt when questioning if we should postpone a medical procedure. It did pay off that year with some other medial issues, from ACL surgery to a vasectomy. (I am withholding names to protect the innocent!)

MIKE: Wow, I did not know our son had those procedures! And I did not want to give her a chance to say "I have had five children by natural childbirth." As I said earlier, I have been to the hospital more frequently, but now of course I can tease her about the phantom gallbladder issue. At least my injuries were documented by hospital equipment.

Also, on the positive side, I spent a Friday night with two of our kids when I was not behind a computer or on the cell phone. Number 3 got to know me a lot better, maybe not the way he wanted to. Our daughter got to practice driving, and we honed her area for improvement: parking. I found out that I was in good health, according to two expensive hospital machines, a doctor, and a nurse.

Most importantly, I reassured my loved ones that I was okay. At least for that night, they could go to bed assured that I was fine. In the words of my daughter, it wasn't about me anymore or my embarrassment that my real pain was not as real as I thought; it was about being there for my family and assuring them I would take every precaution to do so.

I should not be startled anymore when the kids feel free to express their viewpoints with us, good and not-so-good. We fostered that behavior early on for all, even from the time Number 4 could communicate. When he was born, the idea of using sign language with pre-talkers was in its infancy, and we wanted him to have a way to connect and express his wants and needs without having to whine about it. We taught him the basics of sign language that many parents still use today with infants and toddlers.

MIKE: I love how my wife uses "we" here. I would not have initiated sign language. After one of the many books she read or experts she listened to, "we" had to try a lot of things with the kids. Most notable is the time when Kori was in her nesting phase with Number 1. I finally found her at the Kinko's copy store at two a.m. because she had to finish the black and white flash cards she read about after her birthing class. Now they make black and white books for babies, but she had created her own binder with black and white shapes that were appropriate for babies.

After the kids were born they had mandatory flash cards and Mozart time. Even the family cat at the time got mandatory love time with my wife so that no one was neglected. The thing is that she was there to create these programs, but who had to execute when she went back to work? Me. Good thing she wasn't always around to see what happened on dad time, like playing and rock 'n' roll or singing "American Pie."

The annual Christmas photo in matching outfits. 2002

Perhaps we brought this on ourselves as parents when we invited the kids, every year on January 1, at the annual family meeting, to give us "evaluations" as parents.

Let me back up a bit. For more than two decades, I had been getting annual reviews at work. It is part of the feedback loop and compensation plan. At the beginning of the year, you set goals with your boss, monitor your progress against those goals, with a focus on results and not just activities, and then at the end of the year discuss with your boss what you got done. Then you get a rating, as I mentioned earlier, of Exceeds, Meets, and so on. Based on that rating, and company performance, the board of directors decides how much your bonus payout will be, and your boss decides how much you get based on the rating.

The payout is fun, but the process can be filled with anxiety. The employee documents the performance, and the boss comments and sometimes brings up something that happened six months ago that you did not know was a problem; or you find that your boss thought a colleague did all the work when you really did it. There is usually a little incorrect information among all the good stuff.

MIKE: I did not like those times because inevitably she would mope around the house, getting caught up in the one aspect she perceived to be negative when there were so many good things she did. And she wonders why our daughter can't enjoy the moment and celebrate five good things and let one challenging thing go.

Knowing all of this, we decided…

MIKE: We?

…to include a Mom-Dad evaluation process at the annual family meeting. We made an event of it, revolving around food consumption at the critical point in the day so that the kids could talk without the distraction of hunger pains.

We started with an assessment of the big family events over the year: vacations, moves, family milestones. Next on the agenda was "start, stop, and continue." This included the list of things the kids did not want to happen, like my missing their birthdays or making them take the annual family Christmas card picture (always one that makes the list). It also included an innovation platform session for new things like pancake dinners or saving up for a trip to Hawaii.

MIKE: Who calls a family brainstorm an "innovation session"? You can take the woman out of work, but not the work out of the woman. I choose my battles, and she could have this one.

Next on the agenda was the assessment of parent skills for the year, both as a unit and as individuals—Mom first and then Dad. My good friend, fellow mom, and colleague, who was head of diversity and inclusion and who often keeps me grounded, told me that work-life integration is key versus work-life balance, but doing an annual assessment for the family is not what she had in mind. I thought it was a fun way for the kids to be heard and help them get any unresolved issues out in the open. (My wise mom said kids don't work that way, but, of course, I wanted to wrap the year in a neat bow and go on to new beginnings, including any emotional baggage.)

MIKE: Oh, my wife. She keeps trying to push for continuous improvement and closure and someday she will realize that the company dynamic and family dynamic are not the same. While there can be good spillover from integration and alignment at work, home has a more emotional connection, even I, the less emotionally supportive one, can see that. At work, she may spend hours, week after week with colleagues, but she does not live with them, attend milestone moments with them (good and bad), and certainly doesn't sleep in the same bed as one of them.

Feedback always has been welcome in our home. At nine years old, Number 1 took me aside, in a very respectful way, and told me she did not agree with me on the way I disciplined Number 2 after a specific situation. More than ten years later, I don't remember the specifics of the situation, but I do remember my awe at having a very thoughtful, intellectual conversation with a child under ten who was articulating her feelings about it.

Lest you think we have raised the elusive perfect child, into her teens I got plenty of eye rolls and grunts too. In that moment, however, she gave me some solid feedback that made me think twice. I did not change my mind, but I did see her interpretation, which helped me have a better conversation later with Number 2. We consistently apologize to Number 1, saying she has taught us to be better parents, not just because she is the first, but also because she has been a good mirror for us at times.

When the kids were younger, we might hear things at the annual meeting like we didn't buy them the Lego sets they wanted. As they got older, the feedback became more of a reflection of who we were and what choices we made, and sometimes harder to take was the feedback that one of us yells a lot, one of us is not on time when we say we are going to be, both of us should stop arguing with each other, and we tend to be overinvolved parents.

In fairness to the kids, there were a lot of positive things too, but like most of us in our job review, using 360-degree evaluations—a work tool that incorporates feedback from bosses, coworkers, colleagues, and direct reports—and overall feedback, we tended to remember the ones that made us feel the "ouch" factor.

MIKE: This is exactly why I don't ask the kids for feedback. I know I have bad days, but I don't want to share my feelings about it. It was just a bad day, but for Kori, she is always thinking how something will affect the kids and she wants to talk about it. She is worried it will come up six months or a year later.

The kids have come to the point where they label family incidents, kind of like project names. Every year, the red chair incident is on the top of the list. In my defense, it happened years ago, but the kids act as if I do the red chair every day, and I admit here, in public, that I was wrong.

We were all getting ready for a party, and admittedly I got a little more stressed than usual about two hours before the start; I wasn't sure if all I had imagined would get done before our guests arrived.

MIKE: We both love to entertain, but I have to admit that these days I weigh the two days—or often two weeks—of stress and tension that my wife inflicts on the family against the goal of a few hours of fun with friends. Don't get me wrong, I really enjoy the connection with others and the ability to have a few beers and burgers with great company and even better conversation. My wife, however, thinks we can't entertain unless the entire yard is weeded, every piece of yard furniture is washed down, every piece of paper on the kitchen counter is "dealt with," and that we have the right skewers for the shish kabobs she just decided to make not more than two hours before.

As I was cutting vegetables, I kept staring at the red chair that I, two weeks prior, had asked my husband to move to the basement. If I could have moved it myself, I would have; the size required two or more people. It had been on my list of preparty projects for two weeks, and it was still there—two hours before the party started.

MIKE: It was on my list, just not to the top yet.

As each kid checked the list for the next party prep assignment, from filling a cooler with ice to making sure each bathroom had extra toilet paper, they asked about the red chair.

Here is the picture: each child came in at different time intervals looking for the next job, read the list, and then left to do it as the next one entered the room with the list. Each child, one at a time, asked about the red chair and what that project was. Now, remember, I had asked for this chair to be moved two weeks ago, and I had been staring at it as I cut vegetables for the past hour. Rather than nag, I put it on the list, trusting that Mike would let me know when he was ready.

MIKE: Danger zone. This is what my wife and I have come to realize. Her time frame is NOW and my time frame is I will get to it when it is a priority on my list. This is a reoccurring issue. It was still on my list. It would be done before the party, but then this happened.

When the fourth child, who happened to be Number 2, came to me and for the fourth time asked about the red chair, I—in the home stretch of finishing my project plan before the guests arrived—lost it. I mean top of my lungs, yelling BLEEP, BLEEP, BLEEP (this was well after the swearing game). To this day, I feel bad for Number 2 who happened to be in the wrong place at the wrong time. I apologized and continue to live with that moment as the kids remind me over and over with, "Is that another red chair, Mom?" or "Are you red-chair-mad, Mom?"

Like my colleagues at work, it is one of those incidents that stays with you for a long time. Despite all the good you do, you are still known as the red chair mom and will be for a long time. Who knows, maybe they will strike it from my "employment" file, but somehow I think I will be hearing about that one even when the grandkids come and go. Mom-Dad evaluations—do them at your own risk.

Featured in
this chapter: Kori   Number 1   Number 2   Number 3   Number 4   Mike

17

The next time you need to motivate your kids, try explaining how live microbial organisms excrete waste

I often have been accused of not taking time to smell the roses or celebrate accomplishments, always moving forward to the next challenge. Here is my excuse. At 4:30 p.m. on a workday, I may learn about the positive impact of a project I designed. Then at 5:30 p.m. I walk in the door at the house to all chaos breaking loose and find out I am at the bottom of the rung in the house ratings, behind the three dogs, even the one that pooped on the living room floor that day.

MIKE: Well, if she actually got home at 5:30 each night, we might celebrate more. When Number 1 was a baby, riding on a shopping mall carousel, she kept pointing to the next ride she wanted to try. My wife yelled out, "Enjoy the ride you are on now or you will miss the fun." Ha, as if that wasn't the pot calling the kettle black. Good thing I stayed home with these kids to influence them too.

At work one day, I got accolades for a yearlong project in which my vision and plan set a path for six different community organizations to collaborate on a project. It was bold, well-researched, innovative, and a strategy-driven project plan, and I had secured resources for a three-year commitment of funding.

When I got home that night, I could not even get six family members on the same page for a house plan. There have been times when I have handled an angry room of executives without any emotions or excitement, while not more than a few hours later, I was over the edge when our four children were talking to me at the same time and three dogs jumped on my lap to get my attention. In the case of the kids, I really wanted to hear what they had to say; yet they were just all competing at once and excited at all that they had to share.

My entire career has been about managing projects and engaging multiple people to work toward a goal. Maybe not in the official capacity of a project manager, but for a long time I have been in the role of getting stuff done. I have developed a skill of establishing a deadline and working backward, to determine key performance milestones by which to know if a project is on task or not, and I am experienced enough to build in cushion and contingency plans because projects rarely go perfectly on schedule.

MIKE: Always working on the project plan. I am even afraid to ask if she has a project plan for our marriage because she will probably produce one, and then I can't say I had no knowledge of it. Better just to stay in the ignorance-is-bliss column.

At work, colleagues, coworkers, and employees also are vested in getting projects done on time and in many cases incentivized with pay. At home, I have to remember that my spouse is not my employee, and neither he nor our children work on tight project plans. After years of trying to train my spouse to think and see things like I do—and facing frustration at the task—I came to the realization that he would get it done his own way, and I had to choose my battles; would I value a dust-free house over a child interacting with dad? A wise counselor also taught me a long time ago the difference between "wanting something done" and "wanting something done my way."

I also learned long ago to appreciate that there is more than one way to get things done, and to respect that if he thinks vacuuming one room a day is the best way and it gets done by Friday, then for sanity's sake, I had to stop trying to control all. It does not stop me from trying!

MIKE: She has gotten a lot better at that over time. We still don't agree on how things get done, but then when she traveled, she did not see it. I also learned a few tricks of my own. Make sure the first room your wife sees is the most clean and organized; it sets a positive tone for the rest of the mess. Thank you to stay-at-home dad Hogan Hilling for that piece of advice.

With four children, spaced apart in age the way they are, we had entered the era of graduation parties. For me, each new party is an incentive to clean and declutter. We both love parties, and Mike believes I also love all the work it takes to get there. He has told me as much that he thinks I like removing junk, cleaning out storage spaces, and going through kids' closets three times a year to get rid of the old and make room for the new. Let me be clear. I like the end result of a cleaning project, but by no means do I look forward to it, especially when I have to motivate not one but five people to do projects around the house.

Here is a typical conversation when it comes to cleaning in our house:

KID: "Dad, where is my uniform for the game?"

DAD: "I put it on your dresser."

KID: "I don't see it."

DAD (as he enters the room): "Well, I can't even walk in here. No wonder you can't find it. Here it is on your dresser, under the clean sweat shirt and maybe clean underwear?"

MOM: "Hey, how about we work on all rooms this weekend, including ours, hon, and if we get it all done, we can go see a movie?"

ALL IN UNISON (minus Mom): "UUGGHHHH."

KID: "How about not. I don't want to see a movie anyway."

DAD: "Come on, kids, listen to your mom. You all can start tomorrow morning."

MOM: "How about you, hon? You have committed to get the garage and the basement storage cleaned out for the past two years."

DAD: "Well, that is a bigger project than a movie as an incentive."

MIKE: In my defense, every man should have his own place, his man cave. Mine happens to be the garage and the storage room in the basement. She even admitted as much, but I have to remind her often about that admission.

After reading a number of books on organizing, I suggested we break the projects down into small tasks, and I wrote a mini-project plan—really a checklist—for Project House Cleanup. I posted the plan in the kitchen and encouraged the family team to do a task a day and check it off, and we would be done in no time. I built in a two-week window in case any athletic events or surprises came up, and then I shared plan B. If nice, project-planning, incentive-offering Mom is ignored, I would invite mean, yelling Mom to the house to instill negative reinforcements. I didn't want to engage the latter, and neither did the family, but for some reason that was not incentive enough to get the job done.

After taking a mom time-out and recognizing that I did not want to give them another red chair incident, I regained my composure and did the next best thing. I applied the knowledge and know-how that only comes with the experience and the wisdom learned along the way.

We gathered back at the kitchen, and I offered the kids some yogurt. In general our kids like yogurt, and they are always hungry. After they are about halfway through the serving, I told them a story. They rolled their eyes, but they agreed to listen because, in general, they knew I could tell a pretty good story, and the bonus is that it was a real story from my own life when I was in the ninth grade, close to their ages at the time.

I told them about my ninth-grade biology teacher, Mr. Ley. Truth be told, I had a major teacher crush on Mr. Ley. The kids thought that was hysterical that I would have a crush on anyone else but their dad and that my biology teacher was named Mr. Ley. I think Number 3 said something like, "Get it, Mom, biology and lay," as if I was born yesterday. I let them have their laughs.

I continued with the story and said that Mr. Ley shared this secret thirty-two years ago and I remembered it as if it was yesterday. We were studying live organisms. Once again, interruption, because of course the kids laughed because they thought I said orgasms. I let them laugh. I continued, asking them if they knew that yogurt was actually made of live organisms—hmmm, I got their attention.

Mr. Ley said, "Can you imagine it? The next time you eat your yogurt, think about a classroom just like this in the yogurt container you are eating and enjoying as a snack right now. The teacher is at the front of the class, and an organism raises his hand—one finger for number one and two fingers for number two. The organism teacher said, 'No worry, go to the bathroom right here, and the humans will eat it.'"

The kids looked at their spoons, looked in their yogurt containers, and said, "OOOOOHHH gross!" They put their spoons down and walked away, but I had the last laugh.

I said I could use my brain to get the last laugh; I was not claiming to be mature about it. Today, the kids still eat yogurt.

MIKE: I have to admit, it was pretty funny, and it worked. The kids went to their rooms, and I followed up with the checklist for each, not wanting Kori to lose it on me. She had contained her frustration so well that day; I was worried that one more negative comment would have made her burst, and the only one left in the kitchen at that point was me.

Whatever it takes to get the job done, right? We did celebrate that night, after the family completed more than half of the mini-projects, and we were well on our way to finishing in time for the next party. Shortly after that, the project was getting ready for the holidays and relatives coming to town, and then on to the next event to catalyze a little home renovation. Ah, no wonder the family started protesting when I suggested inviting people over for dinner.

Having fun around the house, 2006

This is what they think of my stories now. Teens who love their parents (or so I hope). 2015

Featured in this chapter:

Kori

Mike

18

My continuing love-hate relationship with technology, and my realization that the alarm only works if you take action when the phone rings

I appreciate the benefits of technology, including the all-essential Google maps, which makes up for my deficiency in a sense of direction. It drives us crazy, however, when the kids bring their phones to the dinner table or, better yet, when they text each other and they are only two feet away.

On a cold day in January, it was the ATM, that brought me the most warmth, and not for the cash it dispensed. While admittedly, the bills help me buy stuff that warms me, this time the machine itself reached out, touched me, and made my day. Before you dismiss me for being a crazy woman, let me explain.

Anthropomorphism is the literary technique of applying human characteristics to inanimate objects. I think I learned this in Mr. Filareke's fifth-grade class, and as someone who always has been fascinated by words—so much so that at a young age I loved the Word Power column in *Readers Digest*—

it has stuck with me. The idea that the alarm clock, the shower head, or family car could actually think, feel, or talk gave my modern-day, creative mind something to think about other than the pressure or stresses of everyday life, especially when I was in the midst of a moment. I mean, think about it next time you are sitting in your car, getting angry at the traffic or frustrated that you missed your last turn.

Think what your car would say. "Hey, you think you are frustrated? I am getting overheated, my wheels are hot on the pavement, and I am carrying your tush through this mess."

Before the Apple operating system introduced the talking Siri, there was the car GPS. Garmin owners could set the voice to be a man or woman, and within each gender, a number of accents and dialects from which to choose. I selected the man with the slight British accent for my GPS-crush voice and named him Pajama Joe or PJ, aptly named after a television character that I was fond of at the time—a great dad character of course—and the voice reminded me of him. Mike and the kids often asked me how Joe was doing, and if I wanted to invite him to dinner.

MIKE: Over the years, I have been asked a number of times if I was worried about my wife having an affair on a business trip, and I said no. She is just as happy or happier with her Garmin that provides directions, because she is and will willingly admit to being directionally challenged! I think it is funny that we both get asked about this often because I am a man among moms too! Who else would put up with us but each other?

Pajama Joe got me safely to my destination a number of times, and he became part of the family—that is, until I developed a stronger relationship with the iPhone and car-installed navigation system. Now, Garmin is in the home for devices that we have cherished due to the services they provided our family, but are no longer serving in the most up-to-date way. Mike does not understand my need to provide a retirement home for these objects or why I apply human feelings to our technology—not all technology, just the ones that have been there for me and gotten me out of some of my most challenging moments.

At the time I met the ATM, it was a 20-degree Friday night in January, and I was running late, of course. (This is a bad habit I have to break.) I left the office well after the time I promised my husband I would (5:30 p.m.). I had even set my phone alarm, but I had to get out just one more email on this "it's gonna kill my career" project that was a definite blocker to my New Year's resolution to pursue life balance and happiness.

MIKE: Don't even get me started on her home arrival time! Again, I love my wife. Being on time to a family event is not one of her strengths. She can make it to work, a flight, a meeting, or many other events on time. When I ask her to leave at X time to pick up the kids or be at X, it is a fifty-fifty shot—not good odds if she is engrossed in a project or on a deadline. I love her and accept this about her, but I don't love it.

That one more email turned into three, and inevitably, I left the office an hour later than I intended. As you can imagine, this led to other sources of stress that danced through my head, namely, I am late for my son's game, and I broke a promise to my husband to leave on time.

It is no wonder that women in stressful jobs have a nearly 40 percent higher risk of heart disease, and a 60 percent greater risk of diabetes. This is a fact Arianna Huffington—cofounder, president, and editor-in-chief of the *Huffington Post*— mentions in her book *Thrive*. Huffington continues to hit the point home, writing that in the past thirty years, as women have made substantial strides in the workplace, self-reported levels of stress have gone up 18 percent. Even the millennial generation is at the top of the chart for stress levels, according to the American Psychological Association.

In a state of stress that night, I grabbed all that was on my desk and shoved it in a bag, which I knew would create more work to sort through later. I ran to the car in such a rush that I forgot my coat behind my office door. Without my coat, the icy cold air jolted me to a moment of reason or insanity. @$##! I needed two dollars to get into my son's game. I checked my wallet and confirmed my fears—I needed to stop for cash.

I could not call Mike because I had a well-deserved lecture coming my way about being late, and I didn't want or need that right then. I did make a choice and his speech was a natural consequence, but I was also old enough to know I did not want it.

MIKE: I knew it. I now understand why she doesn't call!

I had to go down the busy main street in order to hit the ATM along the way. Lady luck was not on my side; traffic was heavy. When I finally got to the ATM, there was a line, and when it was my turn, I was experiencing high stress levels. I looked at the ATM screen, entered my PIN, and then it happened.

The ATM screen read, "Happy Birthday, Kori!" and it featured a brightly-colored birthday hat with confetti. The gesture threw me for a loop. I looked around a bit stunned, and for a few seconds thought, "How did you know?" I looked at the security camera, wondering if this was a candid camera moment or if I was getting *Punk'd*, the MTV reality series that involved a hidden camera to play practical jokes on people.

And then it happened again. I smiled at the ATM and felt the warmth of its embrace as if it reached out, gave me a hug, and said your birthday is in two days, but you needed this today. The irony is that it turned out to be the best part of the day thus far. Going into the rush, helped me get out of the rush.

The rest of the story is that I reunited with my family, apologized to my husband for being late—ate crow again and again on that one—and saw my son shoot and make a basket. It didn't make being late okay, because I had a lot of making up to do, but I handled it much better than I would have if I had not embraced that chance encounter with the ATM.

MIKE: I have given my wife lots of grief about her tardiness over the years, but we have more or less come to an understanding. For the most part, I accept that part of my wife that is dedicated to her career and providing for our family. It was a life choice that we made to have me stay home and raise

> the kids. As a result, sometimes she is late for their events, but I am most always there on time. For those rare occasions I need her to be there on time, I tell her the wrong time with no apologies. If the event starts at 7:00, I just say it starts at 6:30. I even put it on the family calendar a half hour early. The kids and I know, but she has not caught on.

There also are the moments when technology advancements are not your friend, and I do use these moments to show the girls and boys how to take accountability, even if it means sharing my bedhead with fellow coworkers and a new business partner. The company I worked for at the time invested in a WebEx system whereby we could connect, both in terms of sound and sight, with colleagues via our computers and built-in cameras. The intent was for employees to have both audio and visual contact to enhance communication, reduce travel expenses, and allow for flex work arrangements. A colleague set up a WebEx call for Friday to introduce me to another business partner.

Due to extensive business travel all week, I fell asleep on the couch when I arrived home at just before midnight on Thursday. I woke up on Friday at 6:00 a.m., logged into my computer, and started working again. I was in such a work flow that aside from going to the bathroom and a quick brush of teeth, I had worked nonstop on the computer.

> MIKE: I saw her that morning, as I was in the hustle bustle of school-morning routines. She looked tired, but the picture of a person glued to her email had become customary in the

house. Long ago I fought her workaholic tendencies, but some people just have to learn in their own time frame or experience moments like this one to make a change.

I looked up from my computer at about five minutes before 10:00 a.m. I realized that I had a WebEx call, but hadn't looked in the mirror all morning. I had no idea what I looked like. Too busy to stop working, but quick on my feet, I decided to just say that my camera wasn't working. I logged on and of course my extremely competent colleague told me to just click on the camera button. My conscience wasn't ready to lie about the camera, and for a split second I panicked. As soon as I clicked on that camera button, I would see what my hair and makeup looked like at the same time as my colleague and the person he wanted me to meet.

It was a consequence of my workaholic tendencies to not take a minute to breathe, wash my face, or brush my hair. I was in my gotta-get-it-done mode. In the split second it took me to decide if I was going to click on my web cam, I did think this would be another good example I could share with the kids about the consequences of making certain choices. I chose to answer one more email, and I had to live with the consequences of prioritizing email over my own personal hygiene—a luxury of working from home that day.

MIKE: On this one, I will give her a break. Between us, we have had plenty of examples to share with the kids about what not do to. I will give my wife credit. She is willing to share hers with the world. Me, on the other hand, well, the kids know what those are.

As you can imagine, it was a hairtastrophe! I am lucky the computer cameras were not high definition, but clear enough to see my hair sticking up in the back, like the scene from the movie *There's Something about Mary*—the one where she thinks the semen on his ear (you have to see the movie or YouTube clip) is hair gel. She puts it in her hair and her bangs stick straight up.

Fortunately, mine wasn't in the front, but the back crown of my head was sticking up like it had gone wild. I subtly worked to correct the mess, trying to make it as smooth as when a teenage boy who likes the girl next to him at the movie theater reaches both arms up in a stretch and then, as his arm lowers, he happens to wrap it around the girl's shoulders. You know the move, right? I got about a 10 percent improvement.

MIKE: Yeah, I used that move on her when we were sixteen at the movie theater. I know the move. Didn't know she knew the move.

At the same time, I used the camera picture to check out my makeup. The mascara had run all over my face and was now filling in the bags under my eyes. As the new person introduced himself, I quickly swiped under each eye to rub away what was there. I know first impressions matter, and all the while I was thinking how I could salvage this moment. I decided to come clean with at least part of the story, and told my colleague and the new person that I was having a bad hair day and apologized about that.

They laughed, and I was relieved. At least if I made fun of myself, it took a bit of the sting away from the first impression. Later on that month, I traveled with the two people to Boston, and as we had a business lunch in the airport, I confessed the entire story in full transparency as we waited for our food to arrive. It provided a little levity, and you know what they say, laughter is the best medicine.

As I shared the story with the kids, they gave me all sorts of suggestions from keeping a ball hat close by to doing the WebEx in the master bath itself so that I could look in the mirror. When I told them they were missing the point, and that it was my fault for getting too caught up in my work and not planning the day well, Number 3 said, "We know that, Mom, but you also told us to always put your best foot forward, and I'd say this time you did not put your best foot or face forward. Technology 1, Mom 0."

Taking time out to have some fun! 2015

Featured in this chapter: Kori   Mike

The midnight bus to Missouri and the life lesson in saving money

19

At times, even I look back on some decisions I have made in the name of parenting and exclaim, "What was I thinking!" I can safely say that I did not put the kids in harm's way, but I learned way more than the intended target of my actions—our kids, who were supposed to observe my actions and have an "Aha" moment! They did, however, have a "Ha! Ha!" moment at my expense.

There is a point when raising teenagers that the infamous budget conversation becomes a dinner table dialogue. It is the one where the kids want something or tell you how they covet a friend's house or new car or they want some money, and the parent launches into a lecture on where money comes from. Contrary to belief, it does not grow on trees in the backyard, at least at our house.

MIKE: I love it when the kids say I have all the money because I pay the bills. Kori is really supportive and tries not to crush me or the kids' view of me, but I can tell she is holding back what she wants to say about who goes to work every day outside the house. I have to tell them that my job is great, but I can't get a credit card without Mom's signature.

With all four kids experiencing the teenage years about the same time, the budget conversation was ongoing. Let me be clear that neither Mike nor I were great at managing budgets at the time, but we wanted our kids to be better at it. We decided we should set a better example for the brood.

Part of the additional money stress at the time was due to our own financial woes, as we had four drivers in the house and were about to add one more. I told Mike that we thought four kids were hard when they were younger, but now their toys were just getting more expensive—four wheels, insurance, and the cost to cover the gray hairs that continually grew on my head from thinking about them behind the wheel.

MIKE: I don't even like to talk about it. Every year my wife sends me the new US Department of Agriculture study that estimates how much it costs to raise a child from birth to an eighteen-year-old adult. The latest figure for two-parent middle-income families is about $250K per child...times four...I need to go lie down.

As a planner, we bought a base-model Subaru car, four years in advance of Number 1's legal driving status. I love the Subaru, but the no-frills model was an intentional decision prioritized on price and knowledge that our oldest would need a safe car in a few years. Not that I am above no-frills; admittedly, I would have liked leather over tan fabric, especially with four kids and multiple dogs.

As it turns out, at the time Number 1 could drive, Mike decided we financially could not afford to buy a higher model and pass it down, so we invested in an older, reliable Chevy Blazer that the kids appropriately call the beast—it's not pretty, but stamina and safety make it dependable.

MIKE: So again, we had to enact what she likes to call plan B. She does not like plan B—she just called it that. I looked at the numbers and had to break it to her. Yes, I had promised her a higher model, leather-seat version, but I also promised to pay the bills and at this point other expenses interfered with her plans. When I asked her this question: "Number 4's team fees or her car?" she looked at me in the way I don't want to see again and walked away.

A few years later, Mike found a good deal on a higher model Outback with tan leather seats, low mileage, and a built-in GPS navigation system. It was just in time to do the car shuffle for the driving teens, and luckily we had the money this time. The only issue is that the car was in a different state, about 320 miles away, and one of us had to stay home to be there for the kids. I decided we could save money by picking it up ourselves. After investigating a number of one-way trips, from trains to flights, I remembered my college days and how I used to take the Greyhound bus from Missouri to Illinois because it was the most economical way to do it. I mapped it out, talked it over with Mike, and arranged for the car dealer to pick me up from the Greyhound station in Missouri.

MIKE: Let me point out a few things here. I did not agree to this plan willingly. I may have been a cheapskate at that point, but not at the risk of my family's safety. For two years, I looked for a good car at the right price and finally found it. Due to kid activities that weekend and the next, both of us could not travel down together. She presented a good case, and once my wife has made up her mind, she is doing it.

At the Greyhound station that night, when Mike drove me there at 11:00 p.m., no one cared that I was a vice president at a Fortune 500 company or that I ran the day-to-day operations for a $10 million charitable foundation. I was just another passenger, trying to get to my destination in the safest, best means possible. Mike protested one more time, but I had my ticket in hand and got on the bus with the other passengers who were getting to their own destinations on the midnight journey from Nebraska to Missouri.

As I observed the passengers, I wondered about their stories; some of them may not have had cars to drive or no longer had a license, and some may be just like me, looking for an affordable way to get to the next state. I felt elated at the adventure, knowing what awaited me, and I felt very compassionate for the passengers, especially the mom who had two young kids, one three-year-old boy and a baby girl under the age of one. I counted my blessings that our kids were in bed that night at home and that when they were that age, we had a van and did not have to expose them to disrupted sleep on the public bus.

I was humbled that I had the means and chose to save money with public transportation, while others rely on the overnight bus to get them to where they need to go for whatever reason. The contrasting scenes from the past twenty-four hours of my life played havoc on my sleep-deprived psyche. Earlier in the day I was at a meeting with other executives, deciding how to invest multimillions in funds and later that night and into the wee hours of the next morning, I was on a Greyhound bus with many people, and for some a bus ticket was all they could afford. I thought of my kids and how they are spoiled as I complained about fabric seats.

The three-year-old boy on the bus made me smile. He reminded me of Number 3 in his younger years when he seemingly had never-ending, wide-eyed energy. At 1:00 a.m., his mom told him to lie down, but he was too excited. After all, his slumber had been interrupted at each bus stop; I saw him in his pajamas when I got ready to board the bus at 11:00 p.m., the same time his mom took advantage of a bus stop to take him to the bathroom while his little sis was asleep on her shoulder. I ended up sitting diagonal from him and probably egged him on when I kept smiling at him.

At 3:00 a.m. she got off the bus with the two kids, and I watched, hoping someone was there to pick them up and give them a hug. I offered to help with her bag or one of the kids, but she was protective—I surmised a good mom, trying to do right by her kids. She spoke with the boy about going to see Daddy. I did not see them once they turned the corner.

The adventure continued. I had to switch buses in a very small town, which required me to wait two hours at a nearby bus station. I had a good book with me, freshened up in the bus station bathroom, and then met a lovely security guard whom I believe enjoyed having someone to talk with that morning. He was supposed to shut the station doors after the bus left, but he said I looked like such a nice person so he let me stay in the station. He told me all about the town history and his girlfriend, and mind you this man was about seventy-five years young. Then at 8:00 a.m. on a Saturday morning, I was the only one on the next bus for about ninety minutes. It was just the driver and me going through small-town America.

MIKE: Again, I know my wife can handle herself, but of course I want to protect her. She loves people and can be quite naïve when it comes to asking people questions and taking genuine interest in their stories. I am surprised she did not give all the cash away that I had given her for her trip. She has a kind heart. She did not need to sit in a bus station at 6:00 a.m. and talk with a stranger, let alone an older man who was probably telling her stories because he had a captive audience.

I arrived at the final bus station and called Mike and the car dealer. The sales agent picked me up and the rest is history. As I drove home in my new used car with leather seats, I thought of all the stories I could tell the kids to illustrate making the best of a situation, engaging with the people you meet along the way, being grateful for what you have, and going beyond the comfort zone of where you live to experience life from a different perspective.

I will never forget that night and remember it every time I ride in my car—the Subaru Outback with tan leather seats and navigation system. My next adventure is an overnight Amtrak ride, not in the sleeper cars, but in the coach section where I can see all the people and create stories for all of them to share with the kids about what a big world it is out there.

MIKE: Not again. By the way, after all of that, Number 1 drove the original, fabric-seat Subaru for about six months before she went out-of-state to school, and within six months of Number 2 driving the car, she totaled the front end. First and foremost, she was safe, but we lost our good driver discount, and then the hunt for another car started again.

Blessed. I may go crazy some days, but this is a great crew. 2015

Featured in this chapter: Kori   Number 1   Number 2   Number 3   Number 4   Mike

20

In the words of Miley Cyrus, "There's always going to be another mountain"

What would you do? You are caught up in the excitement of the first few days of a vacation, one you had planned for close to a year to head to Pigeon Forge, Tennessee, and then walk some trails in the Appalachian Mountains. The first day, you decide to take a warm-up mountain hike that is just short of two miles total. On the way up, it starts to lightly drizzle, but not enough to deter you. Then thunder reverberates among the mountainous terrain, and it sounds ominous in the national park, but you don't see any lightning. Other hikers continue up the trail—again, no lightning—so you figure it is okay. The thunder subsides, but the rain gets harder now. You are just a quarter mile from the top at this point, and the rain continues. Do you turn around or keep going to the top?

Now, what if I said you had eight kids following you on the trail, ranging in age from eighteen months to nine years old?

Most sane people would turn around, but not my fellow mom-friend Dawn and me. Both of us were working mothers of four children, all the same ages in rank order—she and her husband had a nine-year-old and so did we; we each had a seven-year old, and down the line.

We worked to rally the troops, explaining how close we were to the summit, and convincing our respective family members to see our vision of how good it would feel to conquer a mountain today.

We are both blessed to have wonderful husbands who have a high tolerance for our determination yet enough confidence to follow their own lead when they think we are crazy.

MIKE: One of us has to be a voice of sanity in this relationship.

The dads firmly planted their ground in a somewhat tree-sheltered area to provide relief from the rain, tightly held the two kids under the age of two, and declared they were not moving; and really, thank goodness, we knew the little ones would be too young to sense a total accomplishment anyway.

Dawn and I then worked on the next set, our five-year-old boys, who decided to stay with the dads, as did the seven-year-old girls. Now with our first children, we knew we had a chance. At nine years old, they still thought we were cool, and as long as we thought we would all be safe, they were in for the adventure. Off the four of us went, while our wonderful spouses and younger siblings waited at the landing as the steady rain continued to fall.

MIKE: As we watched them walk off, I had a few thoughts going through my head that reflected the miffed foul language I wanted to express: (1) hurry up; (2) we still had the six kids to calm down and walk down the mountain after the foursome made it back; and (3) please let our oldest children be more balanced than their determined moms. And that is said with love and great compassion—at least, all that I could muster at the time.

We made it up to the top, high-fived among us, and then headed back down the mountain to meet up with the rest of the crew. At this point, the thunder was long gone and the rain was light, steady, and cool. It was not necessarily pleasant to walk in, but Dawn and I could wash away the "what-if"—had we not gone to the top—and focus on singing and entertaining our children on the way down to distract them from their wet shoes, wet clothes, wet hair, and overall drenched bodies.

As a side note, there were no injuries, and no one got sick— well, except for our Number 3 who puked when he got anxious, but he did it so often at that age, before any sporting event, that we did not count it. Seriously, no accidents and today it is one of the kids' fondest and most recalled memories when we talk about past vacations.

After we got back to the vans, we opened the back hatches and the kids had a picnic inside while Dawn and I entertained the youngsters by singing and laughing in the rain as they ate lunch, and all returned to smiles and laughter.

As I write these stories, I am going through a lot of rain myself, not only literally as I see the drops pounding against the window, but also in my own life and that of my family. After more than two decades of being a high-achieving working woman, progressively growing in my career and enjoying my role as a working mom, my job was impacted by a large-scale corporate layoff that also affected about 1,500 of my peers. It had nothing to do with my work performance; it was all about the numbers and the competitive environment, and it meant my job as an executive was eliminated.

It was a challenge I did not anticipate and one that took me a while to adjust to, transitioning from sixty-plus-hour workweeks and travel to, well, volunteering to help a neighbor do school pickup when his family had a conflict, and it still gives me angst.

At home, I was in my husband's domain, and, frankly, I did not adjust well. I talked about project plans for the house in anticipation of a graduation party for one of the kids. Now that I had time on my hands, a commodity that I was always short on, I had grand plans to refresh the house.

MIKE: Let's just say after having her out of the way for two decades, it was an adjustment for sure. All of a sudden, I had another human being with her own ideas trying to tell me what to do, and I didn't like it. I love her; I did not like the situation. I sent her to see her sister, visit our daughter, and on other little trips so that she could boss other people for a while. That didn't last long enough, and I had lots of new honey-do lists.

As the breadwinner, some of my identity had left me without warning, but a lot of good has come from this time. For the first time in nearly twenty-five years, I did not have to check my email; I could enjoy a Sunday night without the anxiety of planning for the Monday work rush; I could actually spend quality time with the kids outside of hospital visits or rushing between events to get in birthday dinners. I could help Number 1 move apartments and just lie on her bed when she wanted to do it her way versus my way. In the past I would have rushed her to finish all on the list before we had to drive back home.

I have had time to reconnect with friends and Mike. I have heard and learned from my own parents that adjusting to time together can take some time, effort, and energy. We had not planned on this at this point in my career, and we are nearly fifty years young. The good news is that we have had a mini-trial run for retirement some day, and I think we will be fine.

MIKE: Me too, if she would just not bring out the vacuum all the time.

It also has given me time to reflect on our life and kids. I am very fortunate to know a neat, eclectic group of women; many of them work outside the home and some don't, but nonetheless they have done a yeoman's job of managing relationships, raising families, and pushing through when some things are just not going the way in which it was anticipated.

I have been blessed to be a mom and to experience a great career that will continue and be supported by a committed spouse who made our family a priority, throughout moves, career changes, life changes, and even when both of us did not know what to do or how to manage as parents, let alone parenting in a role-reversal situation.

We are far from done with this parenting journey. As I have told the kids time and again, it is a scientific fact that brains don't fully develop until their mid-twenties, and for some young men, it might not even be until their early thirties. Before this time, they are still young in their ability to process consequences and think two steps ahead. This explains some questionable choices that overall lead to teen pregnancy, drinking and driving, texting and driving, and many other behaviors that are less potentially fatal, like signing a lease that starts in July when the current lease does not end until August (I digress).

These young adults and adolescents are clever souls, and as their vast minds grow, they keep the wisdom we share in a part of the brain that they recall when they need it. When Number 1 recently made a decision that was not deadly or crucial, but maybe a bit costly, she said, "You know, Mom, I am only in my early twenties, and my brain is not fully developed yet."

As I said earlier, I give points to creativity, and while I was not happy with the consequences of her decision, she was right in that we have all made a choice at some point in life that we would not consider to be the wisest one today.

We are still hoping we get it all right with Number 4, but the verdict is still out.

Mike and I have shared some of the seemingly unwise choices that we made as parents, even when our brains were past thirty years old. Reflecting on the thoughts of one of my favorite author's, Brené Brown, these are the real, down-to-earth stories of our life that are authentic, messy, and imperfect.

MIKE: They may be perfectly fine for us now, but at the time, we may have been on the news or featured in the bad parenting moments channel on YouTube—if there was one.

As I said at the start of this book, our intent was not to highlight the working mom, stay-at-home dad family scenario as *the* way to manage, but the way we manage, and more importantly to be very transparent with our experiences so that people feel connected and part of a community if they have a surreal moment or many moments along the way, as part of the parent tribe.

We have benefited from the learnings of others who have gone before us and thought we should pay it forward with transparent stories that made you smile, laugh, and most importantly made you feel that you are not alone. It takes a village for us too. After all, we are still in parenting training for each child we raise—as no one child is the same—and at each new phase of life from infant to toddler and adolescent to adult. Even though we may get more comfortable as we get wiser, a new scenario pops up as each individual makes his or her own choice, whether a family has one child, four, or ten or more. It seems there always is the next mountain to climb.

For that reason, part of the proceeds from this book will go toward nonprofit organizations that supports and brings new information on all types of families to public conversation. For more information on these organizations, see our website, www.ZagZigParenting.com.

Quadruple the trouble and the fun! 2012

We like the zoo. It reminds
us of home. Omaha, 2011

Incredible year ahead.
Christmas Card, 2004

The animals are loose in the Wild Kingdom. Omaha 2006

A safe way for Number 2 and Number 3
to handle conflict—I think? Chicago, 2002

Being goofy with dad. South Dakota. 2007

When they would actually wear what
mom asked them to. 2003

There is always one that
wants more attention. 2014

Before marriage and kids
there was this 1991

Easter. 2004

Kori and Mike

Questions to Spark Discussion among Couples and Families

These are just a few questions to spark discussion with your spouse, partner, or children if you are thinking about changing the family arrangement. There are no right or wrong answers here. It is all about having a shared understanding, and based on our experience and challenges, it is best to come to some agreement on a few things before you are in the heat of the situation.

- What is our family vision (who we strive to be) and/or mission (who we are) statement?

- What are our goals for our kids? Goals for us as a couple?

- What are the core values we have for our family?

- What are the priorities for the family?

- What comes first, the kids' needs or our needs as a couple?

- What will we not trade off?

- When do we want to retire? What do our finances allow?

For the men:

- How will you feel/react if someone calls you Mr. Mom?

- How will you handle the potential isolation from other working men?

- Are you willing to make a domestic decision without your spouse's involvement, and will you be confident enough to stick with it when she may be upset?

- Can you buy tampons at the store or is this too embarrassing for you?

- If you are managing multiple kids or a dealine, do you have a support system close by (family, close friends, or people you can become friends with when the going gets tough) to help you when you need a time-out from the kids or you need other help?

For the women:

- Are you willing to let your spouse/partner do things his way without intervening?

- How will you handle potentially missing a child's milestone event?

- What expectations do you have of your spouse/partner for including you or documenting events for you?

- What "rules" might you think about for kids or your spouse calling during work time or how quickly you can respond during work hours?

- In the spirit of not sweating the small stuff, what is small and what is big to you? Or in the spirit of picking your battles, what is battle-worthy or not battle-worthy?

Kori's Suggested Reading List

For Working Moms

Lean In: Women, Work, and the Will to Lead by Sheryl Sandberg, COO of Facebook, *Time*'s 100 Most Influential People, and Fortune's 50 Most Powerful Women in Business.

- Following a 2010 TEDTalk, Sandberg introduced the Lean In concept to encourage women to lean into their careers versus backing away when debating if-when-how to raise children as a career woman. I appreciate the myriad of facts in the book about working women—the challenges and the benefits—as well as the counsel and her personal experiences. The book led to the creation of the LeanIn.org movement.

Thrive: The Third Metric to Redefining Success and Creating a Life of Well-Being, Wisdom, and Wonder by Arianna Huffington, cofounder and editor-in-chief of the *Huffington Post* and celebrated as one of the world's most influential women.

- Huffington defines success with dimensions that go beyond the typical money and power to address health and wisdom, creating a more holistic definition of what it means to be successful. Like Sandberg, in her book Huffington includes a number of well-documented research studies, intermixed with personal experience and inspiration. She stressed the importance of sleep and relationships and family.

Family—The Ties that Bind...And Gag! By Erma Bombeck, American humorist and newspaper columnist that described suburban life from the mid-1960s to the late 1990s.

- This is one of more than a dozen books she published, most of which became best sellers. I recommend reading all, chronicling the ordinary life of a Midwestern suburban housewife. While these may be dated, the wisdom and humor transcend time.

I Thought It Was Just Me (But It Isn't) by Dr. Brené Brown, a research professor at the University of Houston Graduate College of Social Work and author of a number of best sellers on the topics of studying vulnerability, courage, worthiness, and shame.

- This is one of many books I suggest by Brown who champions authenticity and vulnerability as tools in personal growth versus traits to be feared and hidden. Check her website at brenebrown.com and join her online learning communities: The Daring Way and COURAGEworks.

The Family Manager's Guide for Working Moms by Kathy Peel, called "America's Family Manager," she is the award-winning author of twenty-one books that have sold more than two million copies.

- Peel openly applies business management strategies in her home and has tested them and shown that the blend of worlds can work.

For At-Home Dads

Dads Behaving Dadly: 67 Truths, Tears, and Triumphs of Modern Fatherhood by Hogan Hilling and Al Watts, two dads who are and have been active in the National At-Home Dad's Network. Hilling is the founder of Proud Dads, Inc.

The Modern Mom's Guide to Dads: Ten Secrets Your Husband Won't Tell You by Hogan Hilling and Jesse Jayne Rutherford, a mother, freelance writer, and writing coach.

On Parenting

Parenting with Love and Logic: Teaching Children Responsibility by Forster Cline, MD, and Jim Fay. Cline is an internationally renowned child and adult psychiatrist, and Fay has three decades of experience in education as a teacher and administrator.

- This parenting book (and live training sessions) shows parents how to raise self-confident children, with the use of natural consequences as one technique.

For Spiritual Inspiration

The Bible

- Let's face it, there are a number of characters in the Bible who did not make the greatest choices in life. At the same time there are stories of tremendous hope. Look at David, the youngest child of his family, who defeated the giant Goliath due to his faith and then became king. As an adult, he had an affair with Bathsheba and arranged to have her husband killed. God showed mercy.

Present over Perfect: Leaving Behind Frantic for a Simpler, More Soulful Way of Living by Shauna Niequist, author, wife, and mom, self-professed bookworm and passionate gatherer of people, especially around the table.

- Niequist shares authentic stories of self-discovery on the journey from burnout and busyness to being present and reconnecting with the important things in life.

Unglued: Making Wise Choices in the Midst of Raw Emotions by Lysa TerKeurst, president of Proverbs 31 Ministries and the *New York Times* best-selling author of sixteen other books.

- In the words of TerKeurst, God gave us emotions to experience life and like most women, she has times when others bump into her happy and she comes emotionally unglued. She shares her vulnerable stories on how to shift from a tendency to explode to a deep sense of calm.

When God Winks by Squire Rushnell, American author, inspirational speaker, and former television executive (father of *Schoolhouse Rock*).

- Rushnell is credited with coining the term *godwink*, which he defines as "an event or personal experience, often identified as coincidence so astonishing that it could only have come from divine origin."

To Inspire Transformation

A Path Appears, Transforming Lives, Creating Opportunity by Nicholas D. Kristof and Sheryl WuDunn, journalists, husband-and-wife team, parents, and authors of *Half the Sky* about the struggles women and girls face around the globe.

- *A Path Appears* is a story of inspiring change makers, aptly named because the more people take a path, the more it become visible and others will follow. Kristof and WuDunn cite a number of facts and studies, woven with personal stories and case studies.

The Alchemist by Paulo Coelho, Brazilian lyricist and novelist and recipient of numerous international awards, among them the Crystal Award from the World Economic Forum.

- His novel about Santiago, an Andalusian shepherd boy who yearns to travel in search of worldly treasures, is about the essential wisdom of listening to our hearts, transforming our thinking, and following our dreams.

Family

Acknowledgments

- Mike Becker—husband, life partner, and friend since we were 16 years old.
- Our children—Number 1, Number 2, Number 3 and Number 4—in birth order, not necessarily in favorite status order as you four would expect. (ha! ha!) You turned our relationship into a family; thank you!
- Jill Reed—a strong champion and my mom who passed way too soon.
- Ken Reed—my dad who taught me to use my voice and that my opinion matters.
- Kendra and Kevin Reed—the best big sister and brother who both sheltered me and taught me from life events.
- My extended fam—Kelley, Niece 1, Niece 2 and Nephew 1—LOVE!
- Judy and Bob Becker—although life changed for you two twenty years ago, you raised a son who is a role model of a dad.
- Joe Maida—a friend who encouraged and helped me bring the Daddy-focused children's books to life.
- Steve Noe—a friend who edited early works and encouraged me to continue writing.
- Sandy and Lisa from Concierge Marketing—whose honest feedback helped refocus this book, and rightfully so.

- To all the women who have gone before me, paved the way for women to make more progress, served as role models, and included me as a mentor and friend.
- To all the men who have been role models and supportive toward the progress of all people in our society.

About the Authors

Kori, a natural communicator and storyteller, values authenticity and demonstrates that in her raw, tell-it-like-it-is prose with the purpose of helping people see things in new and creative ways that ultimately build a sense of commonality and community. She is a mom, willing to confess that she forgot the diaper bag if it makes someone feel connected versus alienated at times of self-inflicted inadequacy.

In the face of challenge, it takes vision to see the possible and pragmatism to make it come to life. As Gary Rodkin, former CEO of both ConAgra Foods and PepsiCo Beverage & Foods said, "Kori Reed has the amazing blend of passion and practicality that not only inspires, but actually makes wonderful things happen with a great sense of accountability."

MIKE: As her life partner for nearly twenty-five years, and an experienced dad, I can say that it takes a person who possesses a strength in creating harmony and a stable environment in the wake of her whirlwind, as well as a great sense of humor to handle and balance it all. Over the years, she promoted me from family manager to household CEO as I improved budget skills, demonstrated the ability to take on more duties—from organizing the carpool to the household moves—and successfully led four people through the infant to young adult phases, parenthood with a purpose.

Kori's professional career spans four states and Fortune 500 companies over nearly twenty-five years—most recently in Nebraska as a corporate Vice President at ConAgra Foods, a $16 billion household brand company. In her ten years leading strategic cause and social investments for the company, Kori earned recognition as an expert on domestic hunger, corporate philanthropy, and cause branding. She also served as Chairman for the Association of Corporate Contribution Professionals, a membership and professional development organization for more than 120 peer corporate professionals.

MIKE: I managed four moves, four states, and we added a new child born in each state; this included managing multiple moving companies as well as finding new schools, doctors, and friends who might understand why a man was at home during the day. In Illinois, I was instrumental in starting an at-home dad playgroup, a safe place where, "people would not think the dads were stalking their children because we were watching our own."

Prior to her role in philanthropy, Kori spent fifteen years in corporate communication, earning progressive responsibilities at other Fortune 500 companies—Quaker Oats and PepsiCo (pre- and post-merger) and The Goodyear Tire & Rubber Company. Her communication experience encompassed managing an award-winning, daily, electronic newsletter, coordinating communications during a large company merger, and managing communications during labor work stoppages.

She has been recognized with a CEO Award, Chairman-Award, and Spirit Award at the respective companies where she worked.

MIKE: I have been recognized in a Chicago suburb newspaper for my "Paternal Instincts" and in a subsequent article titled "A Man Among Moms: Stay-at-Home Dads Have Full-Time Reminders of Their Future." My wife also wrote children's books with me as the centerpiece and our family as the subject.

Kori has an innate curiosity about life that fuels her creativity, balanced by a willingness to be vulnerable and learn from others. Reed earned a bachelor's degree in Journalism from the University of Missouri–Columbia and a master's degree in Communication from the University of Nebraska–Lincoln.

MIKE: A degree in marketing from Michigan State University— Go Green!—prepared me to do sales and marketing promotion for the first few years of our adult and early-married life... when I was fighting against what I promised Kori I would be when we were sixteen years old—I didn't mean it!

Married with four children, Kori's favorite thing to do while not in the office is to enjoy the pleasant chaos of the household she and her husband Mike created. Originally from the Chicago suburbs, they currently reside in Omaha, Nebraska, as children, one-by-one, leave the nest to build their own stories.

To book Kori as a speaker,
call 402-884-5995 or
email authors@ReedImagine.com.

Need a Speaker?

Kori Reed is a relatable communicator and storyteller who values authenticity and demonstrates that in her raw, realistic, and reflective sense of humor about managing career and family. Whether speaking with a small group or to a large crowd, she draws from her experience to bring to life the often weird, wacky, and wonderful world of seeking balance while zagzigging through life.

Presentations can be customized to your group, but Kori's most popular topics include:

- **Successexy:** *Redefining a working mom's view of success and having it all*

  In between managing a project on deadline and convincing a child to eat his greens at dinner, the joy of work and parenthood get lost in the chaos and it seem like sexy is gone...forever. The Olympic athletes of parenthood experience the thrill of victory and the agony of defeat in the race toward gold-medal work-life flow. Can we parents have it all? It depends on "it."

- **Couples Conundrum:** *Reimagining male-female roles in the family when society has other expectations*

  When your mom says, "He's a man—he doesn't see that." or "She's a woman—she shouldn't do that," do we let those frameworks dictate our path to success for family? Hear examples of everyday living in a contemporary house where "real" men do dishes and laundry and "real" women take down the outside Christmas decorations in sub-zero temperatures. Reimagine traditional family frameworks in a non-judgmental, positive environment.

- *Momspiration: Reinventing yourself and finding your personal purpose*

  The kids are growing and may need you less. What does that mean for you, your marriage and the next phase of your life? This is a major transformation! What do you do now?

- *Submit to Your Spouse: Reexamining the biblical context in a contemporary marriage and family*

  The verse in the bible about "submitting" to husbands leads to a number of hearty discussions. What is often overlooked in public discourse, however, is the verse a few lines down, Ephesians 5:25. It says, "Husbands, love your wives, just as Christ loved the church and gave himself up for her." How do we rectify the contemporary family in this broader context?

- *Judge Less, Parent More*

  The pressure of parenting perfection is real, and so natural we don't even know we are doing it. Perfect parenting does not exist, yet adequate parenting does not seem okay. There is more than one way to do family; through dialogue we can learn that we are not alone and to support one another.

Family Photo Album

Family, 2016

Thanks Ann Rindone for the great pictures!

Kori and Mike

Family

Visit www.ZagZigParenting.com
for more (Mis)Adventures.